U.S. Department of Justice
Office of Justice Programs
Office of Juvenile Justice and Delinquency Prevention

I0503471

Juvenile Offenders and Victims:

National Report Series

Bulletin

December 2001

This Bulletin is part of the Juvenile Offenders and Victims National Report Series. Published every 4 years, the National Report *offers a comprehensive statistical overview of the problems of juvenile crime, violence, and victimization and the response of the juvenile justice system. During each interim year, the Bulletins in the National Report Series provide access to the latest information on juvenile arrests, court cases, juveniles in custody, and other topics of interest. Each Bulletin in the series highlights selected topics at the forefront of juvenile justice policymaking, giving readers focused access to statistics on some of the most critical issues. Together, the* National Report *and this series provide a baseline of facts for juvenile justice professionals, policymakers, the media, and concerned citizens.*

Law Enforcement and Juvenile Crime

Howard N. Snyder

A Message From OJJDP

For young offenders, law enforcement is often the entry point into the juvenile justice system. When a juvenile is apprehended for the first time for violating the law, it is the police officer who determines the nature of the offender's initial involvement with the justice system.

Law enforcement agencies track the volume and characteristics of crimes that are reported to them. Since some crimes are never reported, however, and other crimes remain unsolved, law enforcement data alone are generally insufficient to fully assess the community's delinquency problem.

Law enforcement agencies, however, also report arrest statistics that can be used to monitor the flow of juveniles into the justice system. These arrest statistics are the most frequently cited source of information on juvenile crime trends.

This Bulletin describes the extent and characteristics of juvenile arrests. It provides arrest rates for violent and property crimes, drug and weapon offenses, and violations of alcohol, curfew, and loitering laws. Arrests and arrest trends for males and females and for diverse racial groups are compared. The Bulletin also details the characteristics of the victims and the perpetrators of homicides committed by juveniles.

Using data compiled by the Federal Bureau of Investigation, this Bulletin offers the reader a wealth of information on law enforcement and juvenile crime.

Most information about law enforcement's response to juvenile crime comes from the FBI's UCR Program

Since the 1930s, police agencies have reported to the UCR Program

Each year, thousands of police agencies voluntarily report the following data to the Federal Bureau of Investigation's (FBI's) Uniform Crime Reporting (UCR) Program:

- Number of Index crimes reported to law enforcement (see sidebar).

- Number of arrests and the most serious charge involved in each arrest.

- Age, sex, and race of arrestees.

- Proportion of reported Index crimes cleared by arrest and the proportion of these Index crimes cleared by the arrest of persons under age 18.

- Police dispositions of juvenile arrests.

- Detailed victim, assailant, and circumstance information in murder cases.

What can the UCR arrest data tell us about crime and young people?

The UCR arrest data can provide estimates of the annual number of arrests of juveniles* within specific offense categories. UCR data can also provide detail on juvenile arrests by sex, race, and type of location (urban, suburban, or rural area). The data can be used to compare the relative number of arrests of adults and juveniles within offense categories, to develop estimates of change in arrests over various periods, and to monitor the proportion of crimes cleared by arrests of juveniles.

What do UCR data count?

UCR data document the number of crimes reported to police, not the number committed. The UCR Program monitors the number of Index crimes that come to the attention of law enforcement agencies. Although this information is useful in identifying trends in the volume of reported crime, it is important to recognize that not all crimes are brought to the attention of law enforcement.

Crimes are more likely to be reported if they involve a serious injury or a large economic loss and if there is a desire to have law enforcement involved in the matter. Therefore, some crimes are more likely to come to the attention of law enforcement than are others. For example, the National Crime Victimization Survey for 1998 found that victims reported 80% of motor vehicle thefts to police, 63% of robberies, 58% of aggravated assaults, 50% of burglaries, 41% of simple assaults, 32% of sexual assaults, and 29% of thefts. Overall, victims reported to law enforcement 46% of violent crimes and 36% of property crimes.

Changes in the proportion of crimes reported may, therefore, reflect more than changes in the number of crimes actually committed. They may also reflect changes in the willingness of victims to report crimes to law enforcement agencies.

---

* In this Bulletin, "juvenile" refers to persons under age 18. This definition is at odds with the legal definition of juveniles in 1999 in 13 States—10 States where all 17-year-olds are defined as adults and 3 States where all 16- and 17-year-olds are defined as adults.

What are the Crime Indexes?

The designers of the UCR Program wanted to create an index (similar in concept to the Dow Jones Industrial Average or the Consumer Price Index) that would be sensitive to changes in the volume and nature of reported crime. They decided to incorporate specific offenses into the index based on several factors: likelihood of being reported, frequency of occurrence, pervasiveness in all geographical areas of the country, and relative seriousness.

The Crime Index is divided into two components: the Violent Crime Index and the Property Crime Index:

Violent Crime Index—Includes murder and nonnegligent manslaughter, forcible rape, robbery, and aggravated assault.

Property Crime Index—Includes burglary, larceny-theft, motor vehicle theft, and arson.

Crime Index—Includes all eight crimes in the Violent Crime Index and Property Crime Index.

Although some violent crimes, such as kidnapping and extortion, are excluded, the Violent Crime Index contains what are generally considered to be serious crimes. In contrast, a substantial proportion of the crimes in the Property Crime Index are generally considered less serious crimes, such as shoplifting, theft from motor vehicles, and bicycle theft, all of which are included in the larceny-theft category.

UCR data document the number of arrests made, not the number of persons arrested. A person can be arrested more than once in a year. Each arrest is counted separately in the UCR data. One arrest can represent many crimes. If a person were arrested for allegedly committing 40 burglaries, it would show up in the UCR data as one arrest for burglary. Also, one crime may result in multiple arrests. For example, three youth may be arrested for one burglary. A single crime with multiple arrests is more likely to occur with juveniles than with adult offenders because juveniles are more likely than adults to commit crimes in groups.

UCR arrest data reflect only the most serious offense for which a person was arrested. An arrest of a person for both robbery and weapons possession would appear in the UCR data as one robbery arrest. The UCR data on number of weapons arrests, therefore, reflect only those arrests in which a weapons charge was the most serious offense charged. This aspect of the UCR counting rules must be taken into consideration when the data are used to analyze arrest volume and trends for less serious offenses.

Clearance data provide another perspective on law enforcement. A crime is considered cleared if someone is charged with the crime or if someone is believed to have committed the crime but for some reason (e.g., the death of the suspect, unwillingness of the victim to prosecute) an arrest cannot be made. If a person is arrested and charged with committing 40 burglaries, UCR records 40 burglary clearances. If three people are arrested for robbing a liquor store, UCR records one robbery cleared.

Knowing both the number of crimes reported and the number cleared in a year makes it possible to compute the proportion of crimes cleared in a year. A much greater proportion of violent crimes than property crimes are cleared.

Most serious offense	Percent of all crimes cleared in 1999
Violent Crime Index	50%
Murder	69
Forcible rape	49
Robbery	29
Aggravated assault	59
Property Crime Index	18
Burglary	14
Larceny-theft	19
Motor vehicle theft	15
Arson	17

UCR data capture the proportion of crimes cleared by juvenile arrest. UCR data also document the proportion of cleared crimes that were cleared by the arrest of persons under age 18. Assessments of the juvenile contribution to the crime problem are often based on this proportion. Clearance and arrest statistics give very different pictures of the juvenile contribution to crime.

Most serious offense	1999 juvenile proportion	
	Arrests	Crimes cleared
Violent Crime Index	16%	12%
Murder	9	6
Forcible rape	17	12
Robbery	25	15
Aggravated assault	14	12
Property Crime Index	32	22
Burglary	33	19
Larceny-theft	31	23
Motor vehicle theft	35	19
Arson	54	49

How should juvenile arrest and clearance data be interpreted?

Considerations in interpreting UCR data on juvenile arrests and clearances can be demonstrated by attempting to answer a typical question about juvenile crime: "In 1999, what proportion of all robberies were committed by juveniles?" The UCR data show that 25% of all persons arrested for robbery in 1999 were under age 18 and that 15% of all robberies cleared in 1999 were cleared by the arrest of persons under age 18.

The key to reconciling the difference between the two percentages is the fact, noted previously, that juveniles are more likely than adults to commit crimes in groups. If a police department cleared all seven of its robberies in a year by arresting two juveniles for one incident and six different adults for the other six incidents, the juvenile proportion of persons arrested for robbery would be 25% (2 in 8), and the juvenile proportion of robberies cleared would be 14% (1 in 7). Arrest percentages are offender-based; clearance percentages are offense-based.

Clearance data are a better choice than arrest data for determining the juvenile proportion of all robberies committed. There are, however, questions about what clearance figures actually represent.

One question stems from the fact that a crime cleared by the arrest of a juvenile and the arrest of an adult is classified by the FBI as an adult clearance. Therefore, some cleared crimes involving juvenile offenders are not counted in the proportion of crimes cleared by juvenile arrest, a factor that makes the juvenile clearance proportion an underestimate of juvenile involvement in cleared crimes.

Another question is whether it is safe to assume that characteristics of robberies cleared are similar to characteristics of robberies not cleared. For example, were the 29% of robberies cleared in 1999 like the 71% not cleared?

A study of more than 21,000 robberies in 7 States between 1991 and 1993 found that robberies by juveniles were more likely to result in arrest than were robberies by adults (Snyder, 1999). The FBI's National Incident-Based Reporting System (NIBRS) data from these States gave the victim's perception of the age of the offender and indicated whether the offender was arrested. This study found that robberies by juveniles were 23% more likely to result in arrest than were robberies by adults. Therefore, the juvenile proportion of cleared robberies was substantially greater than the proportion of robberies actually committed by juveniles. Based on this finding, it appears that UCR clearance percentages overestimate the juvenile responsibility for crime because juvenile offenders are more likely to be arrested.

Arrest data and clearance data can be used to explore different types of questions. Arrest data provide a rough estimate of how many juveniles entered the justice system in a given year; but it must be remembered that a particular individual may have been arrested more than once during the year (and therefore counted more than once), and that a particular arrest may have involved more than one offense (with only the most serious charge counted). Clearance data are more useful than arrest data in estimating the proportion of crimes committed by juveniles, but evidence that juveniles are more likely than adults to be arrested for their crimes indicates that clearance percentages also exaggerate juveniles' actual share of crime.

However, and most important, the trends, or changes, in arrest data are likely to reflect actual changes in the number of juveniles entering the juvenile justice system, whereas changes in clearance proportions can be used to monitor changes in the relative responsibility of juveniles for crime.

How accurate are the UCR-based juvenile arrest and clearance trends?

Annually, the FBI generates national estimates of reported crimes for the 8 Index offenses and national estimates of total arrests in 29 offense categories. The Bureau does not currently produce national estimates of juvenile arrests or arrest rates (although it did produce tables of juvenile arrest rates up through the early 1990s). For those interested in juvenile arrest trends, the FBI's annual *Crime in the United States* reports do contain numerous tables showing juvenile arrest counts reported to the FBI by that year's contributing law enforcement agencies.

Statisticians characterize these annual samples as "opportunistic" samples— that is, each sample contains data from every agency that was willing and able to report to the FBI in that year. The essential problem is that the sample is not scientifically determined; therefore, no one can assume that the sample's characteristics (e.g., juvenile arrest proportions, juvenile arrest rates) are representative of all the law enforcement agencies in the U.S.

For example, let us assume that one sample contained a disproportionate number of agencies from large metropolitan areas or cities. If so, then the arrest tables in *Crime in the United States* would present a picture of juvenile arrests with a more

urban character than the U.S. as a whole. This would mean, compared with the U.S. overall, the data from the reporting sample would have a higher percentage of violent crime arrests, a higher percentage of juvenile arrests, higher rates of juvenile arrests for violent crimes, and higher percentages and rates of arrest for black juveniles across offense categories.

In all, the quality of the juvenile arrest rate trends derived from the sample data reported in *Crime in the United States* is dependent on the consistent representativeness of the annual reporting samples. There are currently no assessments of the representativeness of the annual samples. What is known is that the coverage of the sample has changed substantially in recent years. For 1999, law enforcement agencies with jurisdiction over 63% of the U.S. population contributed data on arrests, a proportion lower than at any time in the prior 20 years.

The traditional approach to the development of national estimates of juvenile arrests (and clearances) is based on the assumption that the reporting samples in the *Crime in the United States* series are nationally representative. The more this assumption is violated, the less reliable are the estimates. It is possible to adjust for some of the known, or measurable, biases in the samples, but this work has not been done. Even if such adjustments were made, the validity of the estimates would still be in question because of the inherent weaknesses of an opportunistic sample.

From a pragmatic standpoint, those who wish to study arrest and clearance trends are encouraged to turn to the FBI's UCR Program and its *Crime in the United States* reports. This resource is the best information available, even with its weaknesses. Users, however, should always be aware of the potential biases in the data and the potential effects of these biases.

Murders by juveniles fell in 1999 to their lowest level since the mid-1980s

The exact number of murders committed by juveniles is difficult to assess

Based on the FBI's *Supplemental Homicide Report (SHR)* data, 15,530 persons were murdered in the U.S. in 1999—the lowest number since 1969. Of these murders, about 1,040 were determined by law enforcement to involve a juvenile offender; however, the actual number is greater than this. In 1999, the FBI had no information on the offender(s) for about 5,630 reported murders (36% of the total). These may have been murders for which no one was arrested or the offender was otherwise not identified, or they may have been cases for which the local agency did not report complete information to the FBI. Regardless, the number of murders committed by juveniles in 1999 was undoubtedly greater than 1,040, but just how much greater is difficult to determine. If it is assumed that the involvement of juveniles in murders without offender information is similar to their involvement in murders with offender information, then about 1,630 murders (or 11% of all murders) in 1999 had at least one offender who was under the age of 18 at the time of the crime.

The 1,040 murders known to involve a juvenile offender in 1999 involved about 1,280 juveniles and 540 adults. Of all murders involving a juvenile offender, 32% also involved an adult and 9% involved another juvenile. In all, 41% of all murders involving a juvenile in 1999 involved more than one person and 59% involved a lone juvenile.

Between 1980 and 1999, the proportion of murders by juveniles that also involved adult offenders increased

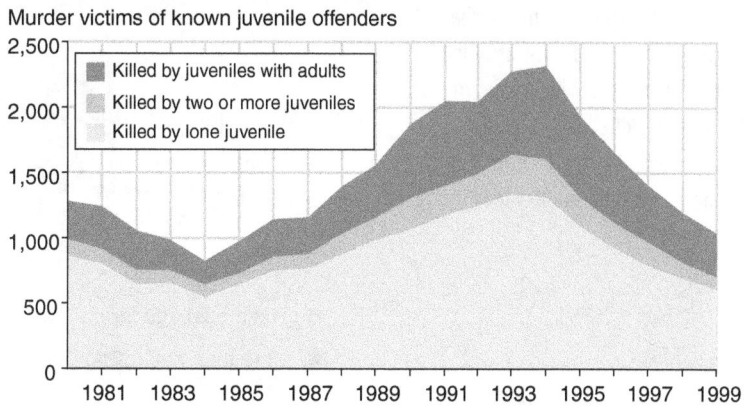

Murder victims of known juvenile offenders

- In the peak year of 1994, 31% of the 2,320 murders that involved a juvenile offender also involved an adult offender. Between 1984 and 1994, the number of murders involving only juvenile offenders increased by 150%, while murders involving both juveniles and adults increased 300%.

Data source: Analysis of the FBI's *Supplementary Homicide Reports* for the years 1980 through 1999 [machine-readable data files].

Between 1980 and 1999, the annual number of family members killed by juveniles did not change

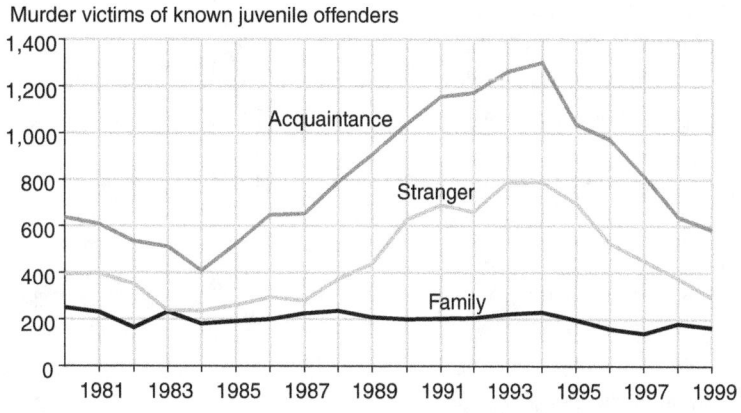

Murder victims of known juvenile offenders

- The overall growth and decline in the annual number of murders by juveniles during this period were attributable to trends in murders of acquaintances and, to a lesser extent, strangers.

Data source: Analysis of the FBI's *Supplementary Homicide Reports* for the years 1980 through 1999 [machine-readable data files].

Whom do juveniles kill?

Between 1980 and 1999, most victims of murders involving juvenile offenders were male (83%). Slightly more victims were white (51%) than black (47%). In 27% of murders by juveniles, the victim was also a juvenile. Victims in 70% of murders by juveniles were killed with a firearm; 25% were murdered with another type of weapon (e.g., knife, blunt object); and 5% were murdered with hands or feet. Of all victims killed by juveniles, 2% were parents, 12% were other family members, 55% were acquaintances, and 31% were strangers.

Who are the juvenile murderers?

Between 1980 and 1999, the large majority (93%) of known juvenile murder offenders were male. More than half (56%) were black. Of known juvenile murder offenders, 42% were age 17, 29% were age 16, and 17% were age 15; 88% were age 15 or older.

Murders by the very young are rare

Between 1980 and 1999, an annual average of about 35 juveniles age 12 or younger were identified as participants in murders—a figure that remained essentially constant over the time period. The majority of these young murder offenders were male (83%), and half (51%) were black. For young offenders, the victim was more likely to be an acquaintance (46%) than a family member (37%) or a stranger (17%). A firearm was involved in 53% of the murders committed by these young offenders.

Between 1980 and 1999, 1 in 4 victims killed by juvenile offenders was age 16–19

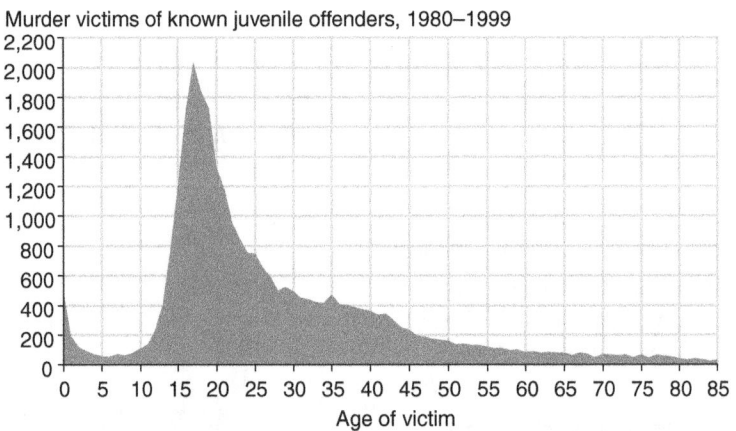

Murder victims of known juvenile offenders, 1980–1999

- The modal age for murder victims killed by juveniles was 17.
- More than half (52%) of the victims murdered by juveniles were between ages 14 and 25.
- Of all persons murdered by juvenile offenders, 9% were over age 50.

Data source: Analysis of the FBI's *Supplementary Homicide Reports* for the years 1980 through 1999 [machine-readable data files].

Between 1980 and 1999, a juvenile offender participated in 47% of the murders of 14-year-olds—the age group with the greatest proportion of juvenile-involved murders

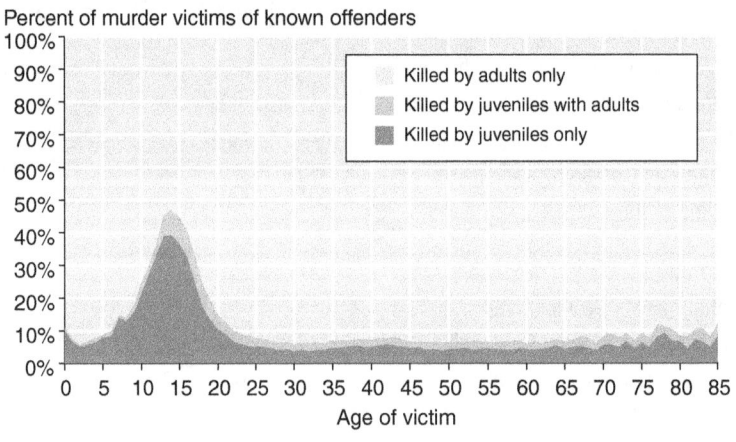

Percent of murder victims of known offenders

- Between 1980 and 1999, fewer than 10% of murder victims ages 23 through 76 were killed by a juvenile.

Data source: Analysis of the FBI's *Supplementary Homicide Reports* for the years 1980 through 1999 [machine-readable data files].

Males—not females—drove the trends in murders by juveniles between 1980 and 1999

Known juvenile murder offenders

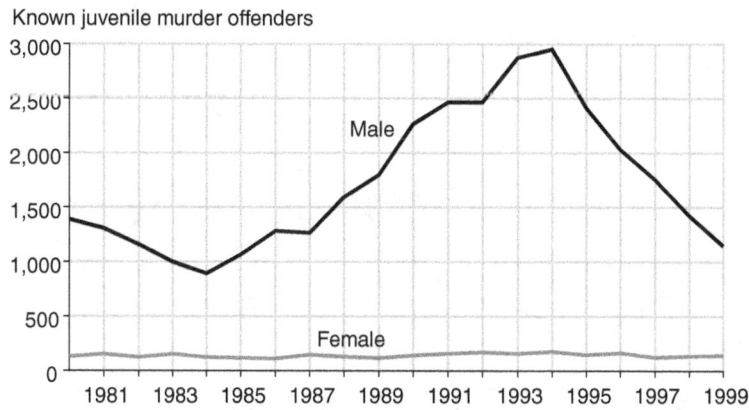

■ Between 1980 and 1999, 93% of known juvenile murder offenders were male.

■ Throughout this period, females were never more than 13% of known juvenile murder offenders. The 13% peak was in 1983.

Data source: Analysis of the FBI's *Supplementary Homicide Reports* for the years 1980 through 1999 [machine-readable data files].

The numbers of white and black juvenile murder offenders were equal between 1980 and 1986—a circumstance that did not occur again until 1998

Known juvenile murder offenders

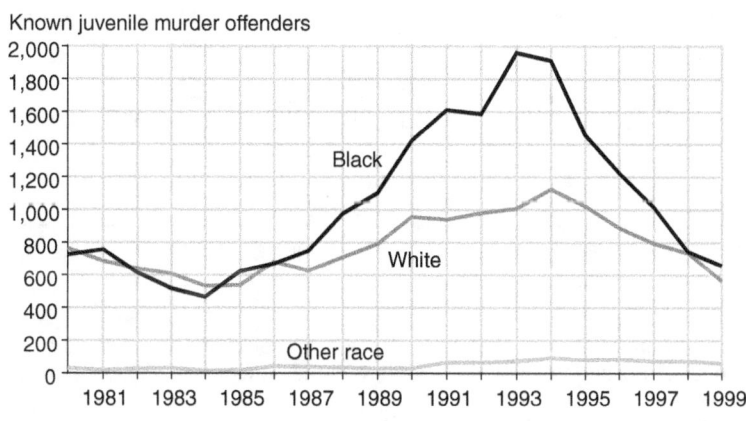

■ Between 1986 and 1994, the number of white juvenile murder offenders increased 64%, compared with 185% for blacks.

■ By 1999, the numbers of white and black juvenile murder offenders had nearly fallen back to their 1985 levels.

Data source: Analysis of the FBI's *Supplementary Homicide Reports* for the years 1980 through 1999 [machine-readable data files].

Boys and girls tend to kill different types of victims

Between 1980 and 1999, 55% of male juvenile murder offenders killed an acquaintance, 37% killed a stranger, and 9% killed a family member. Compared with males, female juvenile murder offenders were far more likely to kill family members (39%) and less likely to kill strangers (15%) or acquaintances (46%).

Between 1980 and 1999, about 2% of male offenders killed persons under age 6, while 21% of female offenders killed young children. Because there were so many more male offenders than female offenders, however, roughly equal numbers of male and female juvenile offenders were involved in the murder of young children. Annually between 1980 and 1999, 10% of male and 12% of female juvenile offenders were involved in the death of a person age 50 or older.

Males were far more likely than females to kill with a firearm. Between 1980 and 1999, 72% of male juvenile murder offenders used a firearm, while 13% used a knife. In contrast, 38% of female juvenile murder offenders used a firearm, and 29% used a knife.

1 in 5 juvenile murder offenders kills a person of another race

Youth were most likely to kill persons of their own race. Between 1980 and 1999, 82% of juvenile murder offenders were involved in murders of persons of their own race. Same-race killing was most common for white youth (90%) and less common for blacks (77%), Asian/Pacific Islanders (59%), and American Indians (45%).

Overall, female offenders were more likely than males to kill within their own race (90% vs. 81%). Proportions of same-race murder victims were similar for white male and female juvenile offenders (90% and 91%, respectively) but differed for black male and female offenders (76% and 90%, respectively).

Between 1980 and 1999, 76% of black juvenile murder offenders used a firearm in their crimes. This proportion was lower for Asian/Pacific Islander (71%), white (62%), and American Indian (48%) youth.

A greater proportion of white and American Indian youth killed family members than did youth of other races: white (16%), American Indian (16%), black (7%), and Asian/Pacific Islander (7%).

Older juveniles are more likely than younger juveniles to commit murders with others

Between 1980 and 1999, 50% of all juvenile murder offenders acted alone, while 20% committed their acts with other juveniles and 30% with adults. Older offenders were more likely than younger offenders to commit their acts with adults.

Age of offender	Percent of juvenile murder offenders		
	Acted alone	With juveniles	With adults
Total	50%	20%	30%
<12	79	13	8
12	69	20	12
13	57	26	17
14	50	27	23
15	48	25	27
16	49	22	29
17	50	16	34

Note: Detail may not total 100% because of rounding.

The overall trend in murders by juveniles between 1980 and 1999 is all firearm related

Known juvenile murder offenders

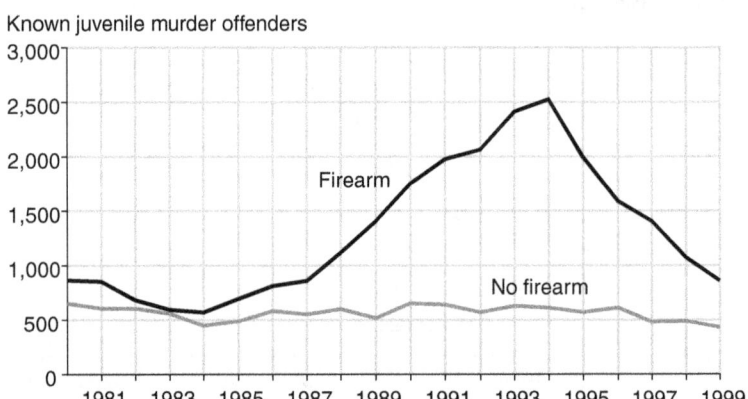

- In 1983, the number of juveniles who killed with a firearm was roughly equal to the number who killed using all other instruments (e.g., knives, clubs, fists, feet).

- In the peak year of 1994, 81% of juvenile murder offenders killed with a firearm.

- In 1999, 67% of juvenile murder offenders killed with a firearm.

Data source: Analysis of the FBI's *Supplementary Homicide Reports* for the years 1980 through 1999 [machine-readable data files].

Firearm use increased between 1980 and 1994 for white, black, and male juvenile murder offenders but not for females

Percent of known juvenile murder offenders

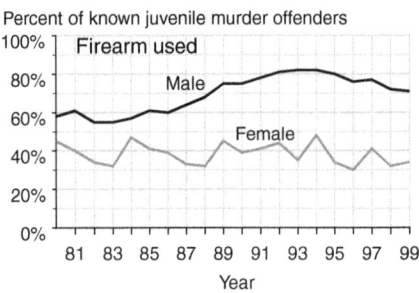

Percent of known juvenile murder offenders

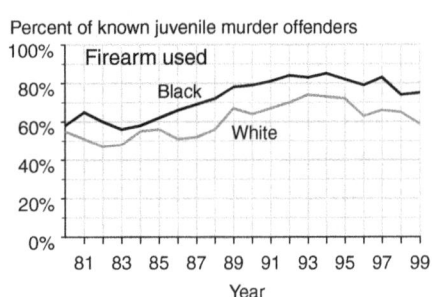

- Each year from 1980 to 1999, juvenile male murder offenders were more likely than female offenders to use a firearm, with the gender disparity increasing in the 1990s.

- Each year from 1980 to 1999, black juvenile murder offenders were more likely than white offenders to use a firearm.

Data source: Analysis of the FBI's *Supplementary Homicide Reports* for the years 1980 through 1999 [machine-readable data files].

Law enforcement agencies in the U.S. made 2.5 million arrests of persons under age 18 in 1999

The most serious charge in almost half of all juvenile arrests in 1999 was one of the following offenses: larceny-theft, simple assault, drug abuse violation, disorderly conduct, or curfew violation

Most serious offense charged	1999 juvenile arrest estimates	Percent of total juvenile arrests					
		Female	Under age 15	White	Black	American Indian	Asian
Total	2,468,800	27%	32%	72%	25%	1%	2%
Violent Crime Index	103,900	17	33	57	41	1	2
Murder and nonnegligent manslaughter	1,400	8	12	47	49	2	2
Forcible rape	5,000	2	38	63	35	1	1
Robbery	28,000	9	26	43	54	1	2
Aggravated assault	69,600	22	36	62	35	1	2
Property Crime Index	541,500	29	39	69	27	1	2
Burglary	101,000	11	38	73	24	1	2
Larceny-theft	380,500	36	40	70	26	2	2
Motor vehicle theft	50,800	16	26	57	39	1	3
Arson	9,200	11	67	80	18	1	1
Other (simple) assaults	237,300	30	43	65	32	1	1
Forgery and counterfeiting	7,000	37	13	78	20	1	2
Fraud	13,100	29	22	57	41	1	2
Embezzlement	1,700	48	6	63	34	0	2
Stolen property (buying, receiving, possessing)	29,100	13	27	59	38	1	2
Vandalism	119,500	12	44	82	16	1	1
Weapons (carrying, possessing, etc.)	42,500	9	32	68	30	1	2
Prostitution and commercialized vice	1,300	54	14	58	40	1	2
Sex offenses (except forcible rape and prostitution)	16,600	8	51	73	26	1	1
Drug abuse violations	198,400	14	16	69	29	1	1
Gambling	1,200	4	11	16	81	0	2
Offenses against family and children	10,100	38	35	76	21	1	3
Driving under the influence	23,000	17	3	92	5	2	1
Liquor law violations	165,700	31	10	92	5	3	1
Drunkenness	21,700	20	13	91	8	1	1
Disorderly conduct	176,200	28	37	67	31	1	1
Vagrancy	2,400	19	20	75	23	2	1
All other offenses (except traffic)	434,100	25	28	74	23	1	2
Suspicion	1,900	22	29	72	27	0	1
Curfew and loitering law violations	170,000	30	28	72	25	1	1
Runaways	150,700	59	39	77	18	1	4
U.S. population ages 10–17	31,321,307	49	62	79	16	1	4

- Although black youth accounted for 16% of the juvenile population in 1999, they were involved in 54% of juvenile arrests for robbery and 49% of juvenile arrests for murder.

- Females accounted for the majority of juvenile arrests for running away from home (59%) and prostitution (54%).

Notes: UCR data do not distinguish the ethnic group Hispanic; Hispanics may be of any race. In 1999, 91% of Hispanics ages 10–17 were classified racially as white. Detail may not add to totals because of rounding.

Data source: Analyses of data presented in the FBI's *Crime in the United States 1999* (Washington, DC: U.S. Government Printing Office, 2000). National estimates of juvenile arrests were developed using FBI estimates of total arrests and juvenile arrest proportions in the reporting sample.

In 1999, approximately 1 in 6 arrests made by law enforcement agencies involved a juvenile

Juveniles accounted for 33% of all burglary arrests in 1999, 25% of robbery arrests, 24% of weapons arrests, 9% of murder arrests, and 13% of drug arrests

Most serious offense charged	Juvenile arrests as a percent of total arrests						
	All persons	Males	Females	Whites	Blacks	American Indians	Asians
Total	**17%**	**16%**	**22%**	**18%**	**15%**	**18%**	**26%**
Violent Crime Index	16	16	17	16	17	17	21
Murder and nonnegligent manslaughter	9	10	6	10	9	15	17
Forcible rape	17	17	26	17	16	16	20
Robbery	25	26	22	25	25	30	36
Aggravated assault	14	14	16	14	14	15	18
Property Crime Index	32	33	32	34	28	38	43
Burglary	33	34	29	35	28	43	44
Larceny-theft	31	31	32	33	27	36	41
Motor vehicle theft	35	35	37	37	33	43	50
Arson	54	55	43	57	41	52	63
Other (simple) assaults	18	16	24	18	18	16	22
Forgery and counterfeiting	6	7	6	8	4	9	9
Fraud	4	4	2	3	4	5	8
Embezzlement	10	10	10	10	10	6	16
Stolen property (buying, receiving, possessing)	23	24	19	25	21	33	39
Vandalism	42	44	33	46	29	37	49
Weapons (carrying, possessing, etc.)	24	24	29	27	19	33	39
Prostitution and commercialized vice	1	2	1	1	1	2	1
Sex offenses (except forcible rape and prostitution)	18	18	19	17	21	11	14
Drug abuse violations	13	13	10	14	10	20	19
Gambling	12	13	4	6	15	17	5
Offenses against family and children	7	5	11	7	4	5	9
Driving under the influence	1	1	2	2	1	2	2
Liquor law violations	24	21	34	26	10	23	26
Drunkenness	3	3	5	4	2	2	5
Disorderly conduct	27	25	33	27	26	20	31
Vagrancy	8	8	8	11	4	4	11
All other offenses (except traffic)	11	11	14	13	8	9	16

- In 1999, 95% of all arrests involved persons between the ages of 10 and 49. Persons ages 10–17 made up 20% of this segment of the population. Therefore, based on their representation in this population, juveniles were disproportionately involved in arrests for arson, vandalism, motor vehicle theft, burglary, larceny-theft, disorderly conduct, robbery, and weapons law violations. In contrast, juveniles were underrepresented in arrests for murder, aggravated assault, forcible rape, and drug abuse violations.

- A greater proportion of female arrests involved a juvenile (22%) than did male arrests (16%). Juveniles were involved in a larger proportion of female arrests than male arrests for liquor law violations (34% vs. 21%), disorderly conduct (33% vs. 25%), and simple assaults (24% vs. 16%).

- A greater proportion of white arrests involved a juvenile (18%) than did black arrests (15%). Juveniles accounted for a larger proportion of white arrests than black arrests for vandalism (46% vs. 29%), burglary (35% vs. 28%), larceny-theft (33% vs. 27%), weapons law violations (27% vs. 19%), and liquor law violations (26% vs. 10%).

Data source: Adaptation of the FBI's *Crime in the United States 1999* (Washington, DC: U.S. Government Printing Office, 2000).

The female percentage of juvenile arrests increased over the last two decades in most offense categories

Gender-specific factors appear to influence juvenile arrest trends

If juvenile males and juvenile females were contributing equally to an arrest trend, then the female proportion of juvenile arrests would remain constant. If, however, the female proportion changes, then the female trend is different from the male trend—and a complete explanation of juvenile arrest patterns (and, by inference, of juvenile crime trends) must incorporate factors that affect males and females differently.

For example, a major story of the last decade was the rise and fall of juvenile Violent Crime Index arrests. During this period, the female percentage of juvenile arrests for violent crimes grew almost continuously—from 10% in 1980 to 17% in 1999. Thus, between 1980 and 1999, while both the male and female Violent Crime Index arrest rates rose and then fell, the female rate rose proportionately more and then fell proportionately less than the male rate. This implies that gender-specific factors were influencing these differential changes in male and female violent crime arrest rates.

Differential growth in aggravated assault arrests helps to explain overall violence trends

Over the last two decades, the female proportion of juvenile robbery arrests increased marginally (from 7% in 1980 to 9% in 1999), while the female proportion of aggravated assault arrests grew substantially (from 15% in 1980 to 22% in 1999). Similarly, the female proportion

Between 1980 and 1999, the female percentage of juvenile violent crime arrests increased, with the overall increase tied mainly to aggravated assault arrests

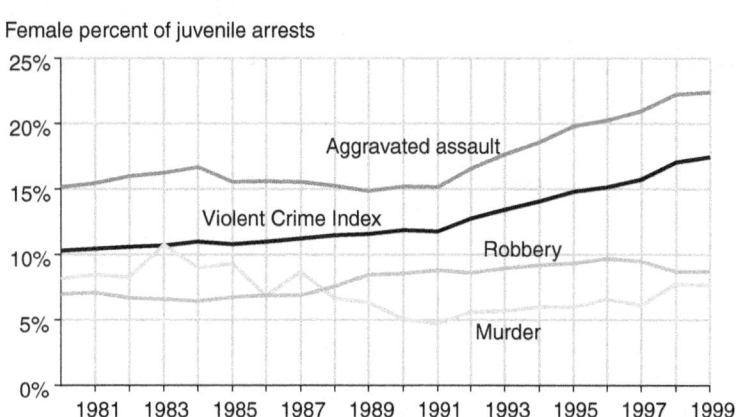

Female percent of juvenile arrests

The female percentage of juvenile arrests increased between 1980 and 1999 for each of the four Property Crime Index offenses

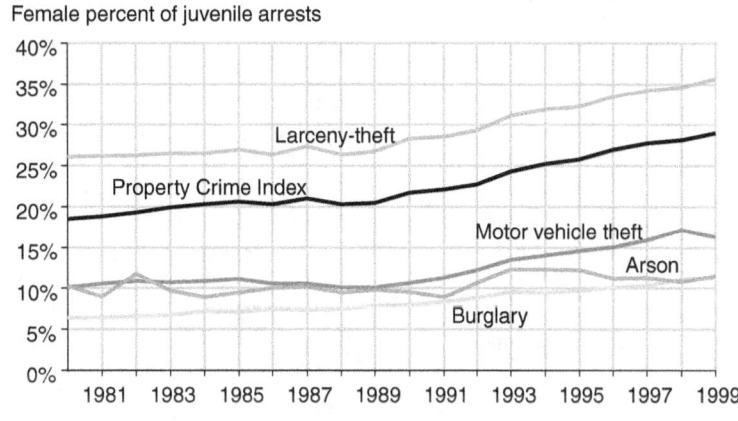

Female percent of juvenile arrests

Data source: Analysis of the FBI's *Crime in the United States* reports for the years 1980 through 1999 (Washington, DC: U.S. Government Printing Office, 1981 through 2000, respectively).

of simple assault arrests also increased considerably (from 21% in 1980 to 30% in 1999). If juvenile females were becoming more violent as compared with males, it would seem reasonable that their arrest percentage should have increased disproportionately for both robberies and assaults. But it was only

in assaults that the percentage increased disproportionately.

A possible (though not the only) explanation for this phenomenon is the changing response of law enforcement to domestic violence. Domestic assaults represent a larger proportion of female violence than

Between 1980 and 1999, the female proportion of juvenile arrests increased for simple assault, vandalism, weapons, liquor law violations, and curfew and loitering law violations

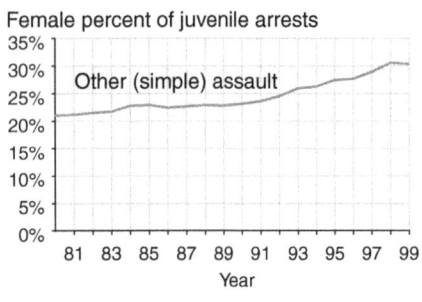

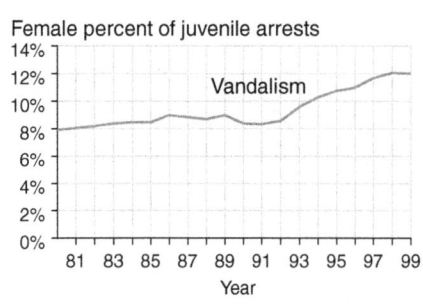

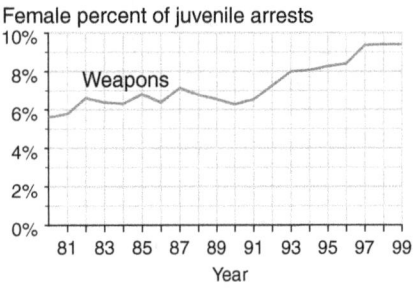

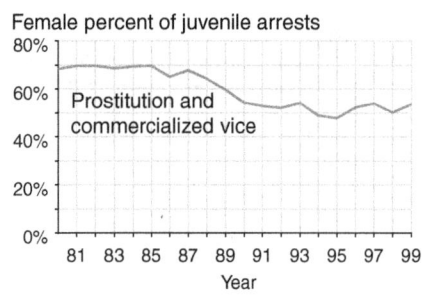

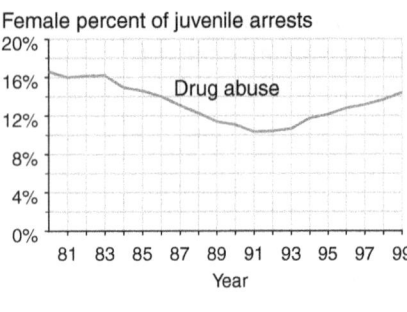

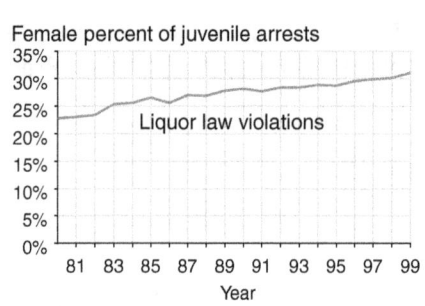

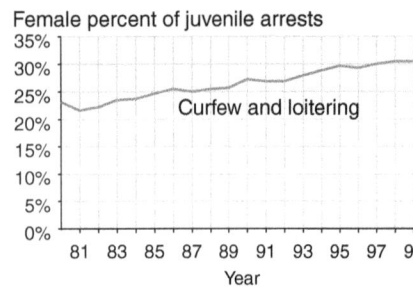

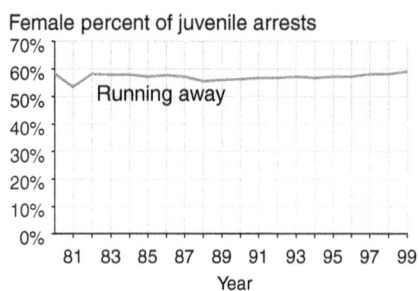

■ Although the raw numbers are relatively small, the female proportion of juvenile arrests for prostitution and commercialized vice did drop substantially between 1980 and 1999.

■ Across the period, females represented the majority of juveniles arrested for running away from home.

Data source: Analysis of the FBI's *Crime in the United States* reports for the years 1980 through 1999 (Washington, DC: U.S. Government Printing Office, 1981 through 2000, respectively).

male violence. Mandatory arrest laws for domestic incidents, coupled with an increased willingness of citizens to report these incidents to authorities and of law enforcement to intervene, would yield a greater increase in female than male arrests for assault, while having no effect on robbery. Thus, policy and social changes may have driven the consistent increase in the female proportion of juvenile violent crime arrests over the last two decades—a period when overall juvenile violence first increased then declined.

Other patterns may give clues to factors driving female arrest trends

When male and female juvenile arrest rate trends move together (increasing, decreasing, or remaining the same), the factors behind the overall juvenile arrest rate trends appear to have no unique, gender-specific component. One offense for which this was true over the last two decades (i.e., an offense for which the female proportion held constant) was running away from home.

Other arrest trends imply that gender-specific factors were at work. From 1980 through 1999, female arrest percentages increased for most offenses, including assault, larceny-theft, vandalism, weapons law violations, liquor law violations, and curfew and loitering law violations. The female proportion of juvenile arrests for drug abuse violations declined from 1980 through the early 1990s and then increased through the remainder of the 1990s. The only other offense for which the female proportion of juvenile arrests dropped during the 1980s and 1990s was prostitution, falling from near 70% in the early 1980s to below 50% in the mid-1990s.

Public policy in the last two decades was driven by concerns about the rise in juvenile violence

Violent crime arrest rates declined after 1994

Between 1980 and 1988, the juvenile Violent Crime Index arrest rate was essentially constant. After these years of stability, the rate grew by more than 60% in the 6-year period between 1988 and 1994. This unsettling and rapid growth triggered speculation about changes in the nature of juvenile offenders—concerns that spurred State legislators to pass laws that facilitated an increase in the flow of these youth into the adult justice system. After 1994, however, the violent crime arrest rate fell. In the 5 years between 1994 and 1999, the rate fell more than 50%, to just about the average of the early 1980s.

Female violent crime arrest rates remain relatively high

In 1980, the juvenile male violent crime arrest rate was eight times greater than the female rate. By 1999, the male rate was just four times greater. This convergence of male and female arrest rates is due to the large relative increase in the female rate. Between 1980 and 1994, the male rate increased 50%, while the female rate increased 117%. By 1999, the male rate had dropped to 7% below its 1980 level, while the female violent crime arrest rate was still 74% above its 1980 level.

Arrest rates declined for all racial groups

All racial groups experienced large increases in their juvenile violent crime arrest rates in the late 1980s and early 1990s, followed by declines through

After a decade of substantial growth and decline, the 1999 juvenile violent crime arrest rate returned to the level of the 1980s

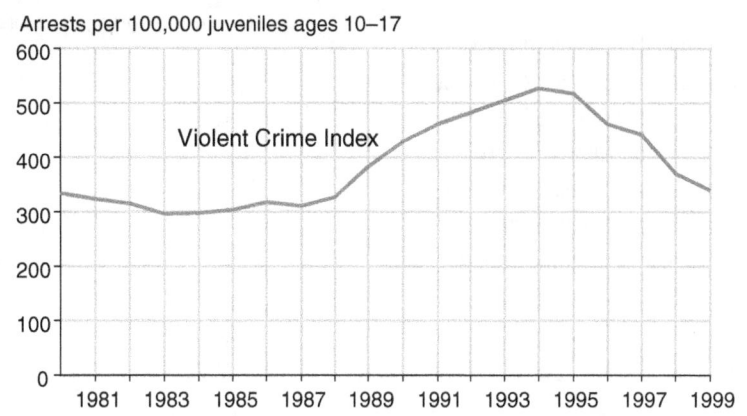

Violent Crime Index arrest rate trends by gender and race

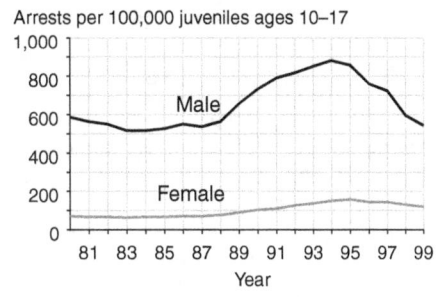
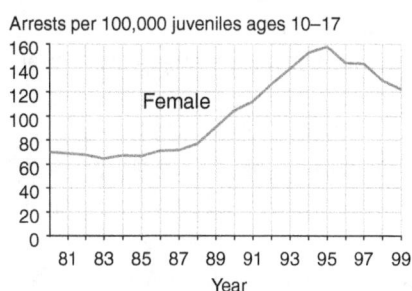
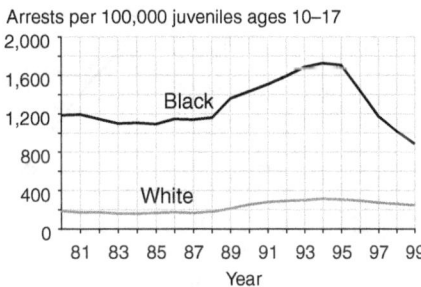
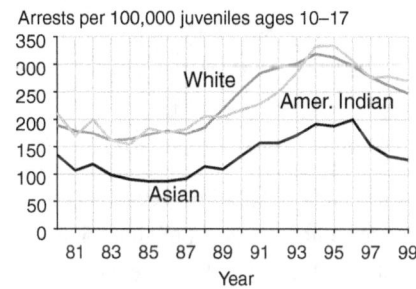

Data source: Analysis of arrest data from the FBI and population data from the U.S. Bureau of the Census. [See arrest rate data source note on page 32 for details.]

1999. However, the fall was more precipitous for black juveniles. The black rate in 1999 was 25% below its 1980 level, while the white and American Indian rates in 1999 were still about 30% above their 1980 levels.

The era of extraordinary rates of juvenile murder arrests appears to have ended

The 1999 juvenile murder arrest rate was the lowest in 20 years

Between the mid-1980s and the peak in 1993, the juvenile arrest rate for murder more than doubled. After 1993, the rate fell continuously; by 1999, it was below the rates of the early 1980s. Fewer juveniles were arrested for murder in 1999 than at any time in at least the prior 20 years.

Male arrests drove murder arrest rate trends

During the 1980s and 1990s, the juvenile male arrest rate for murder was, on average, about 13 times greater than the female rate. Both displayed generally similar trends. The female arrest rate peaked in 1993 at 62% above its 1980 level, whereas the male rate peaked at 129% above the 1980 rate. Both fell after 1993, so that by 1999, both arrest rates were substantially below their levels of the early 1980s.

The rise and fall of juvenile murder arrest rates were linked to the arrests of black juveniles

The black-to-white ratio of juvenile arrest rates for murder grew from about 5 to 1 in 1980 to 9 to 1 in 1993, reflecting the greater increase in the black rate over this period—the white rate increased 50% while the black rate increased more than 200%. Both rates fell from 1993 through 1999, with the black rate falling considerably more, so that in 1999, the black-to-white arrest rate ratio was once again 5 to 1 and both rates were at their lowest levels in two decades.

The juvenile arrest rate for murder in 1993 was three times greater than the rate in 1999

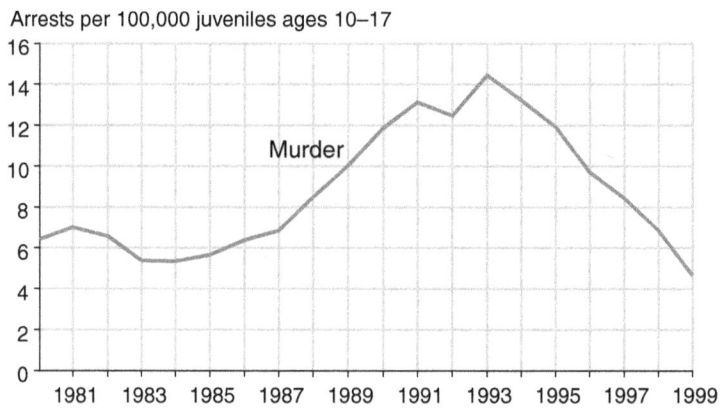

Arrests per 100,000 juveniles ages 10–17

Murder arrest rate trends by gender and race

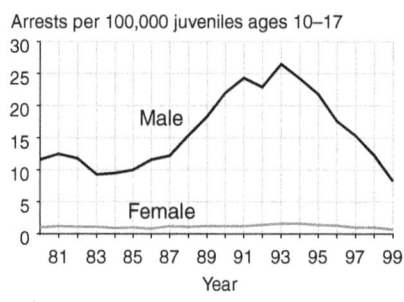

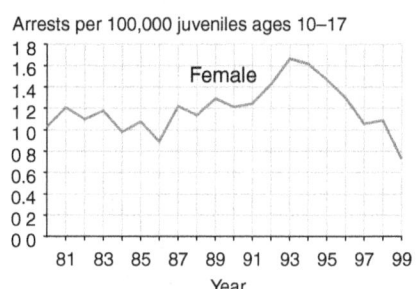

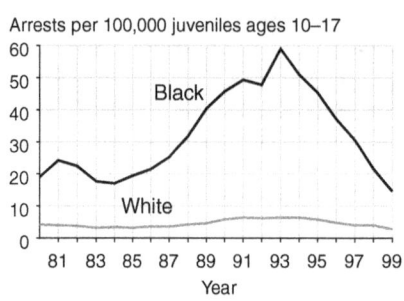

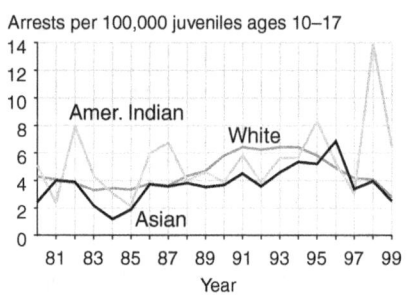

■ Over these two decades, the black juvenile arrest rate for murder increased and then decreased more dramatically than did the arrest rates for other races.

■ By 1999, the murder arrest rates for both genders and all races of juveniles had returned to the levels of the early 1980s.

Note: The annual murder arrest rates for American Indians fluctuate because of the small number of arrests, but the average rate over the period is close to the white rate.

Data source: Analysis of arrest data from the FBI and population data from the U.S. Bureau of the Census. [See arrest rate data source note on page 32 for details.]

Forcible rape arrests indicate a decline in sexual offenders entering the juvenile justice system

The juvenile arrest rate for forcible rape in 1999 was near its lowest level in two decades

Between 1980 and the peak in 1991, the juvenile arrest rate for forcible rape increased 45%. This growth occurred during a time when there were also increases in arrest rates for aggravated assault and murder. After 1991, the forcible rape arrest rate gradually fell, returning in 1999 to a rate near those of the early 1980s.

Black rates fell while white rates rose

In 1980, the black juvenile arrest rate for forcible rape was more than seven times the white rate; by 1999, this ratio had fallen to less than 3 to 1. This was attributable to the 41% decline in the black rate and 57% increase in the white rate over this period.

Forcible rape is just one aspect of violent sexual assault

An analysis of violent sexual assault incidents using the 1991–96 data files from the FBI's National Incident-Based Reporting System found that 45% of all violent sexual assaults were forcible rapes, 42% were forcible fondlings, 8% were forcible sodomies, and 4% were sexual assaults with an object (Snyder, 2000). In these data, two-thirds of all victims of violent sexual assaults were under age 18, and half of these were under age 12. Juvenile offenders assaulted 4% of adult victims but 40% of victims under age 6.

The juvenile arrest rate for forcible rape declined throughout most of the 1990s, with the rate falling far more for blacks than whites

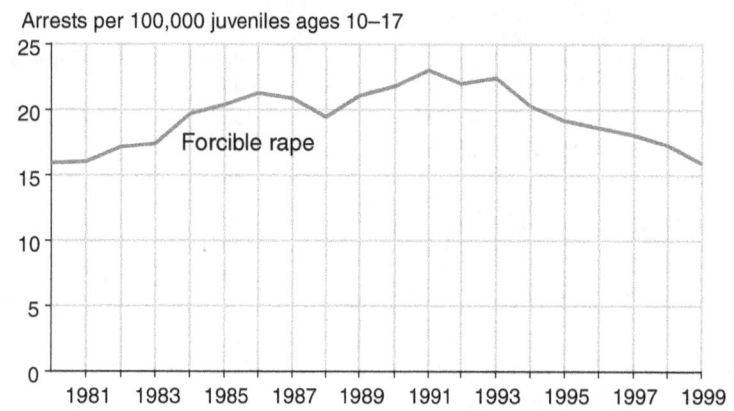

Forcible rape arrest rate trends by gender and race

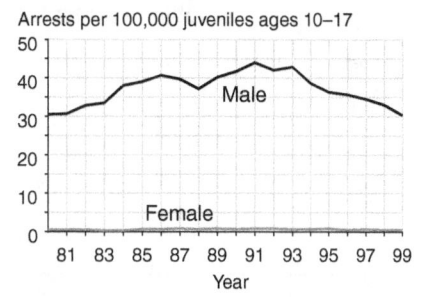
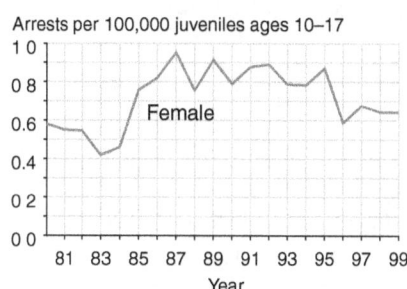

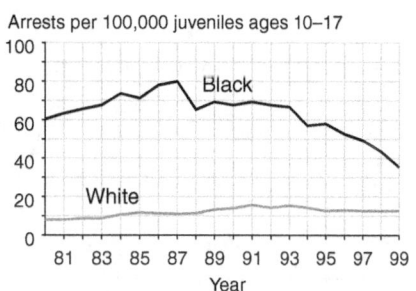
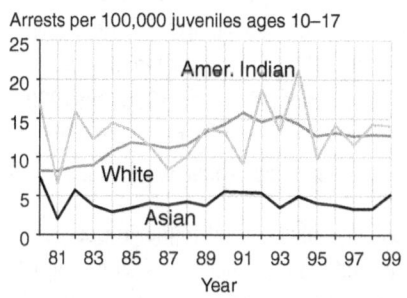

■ After 1993, the sharp decline in the black juvenile arrest rate for forcible rape stands in stark contrast to the relative stability of the juvenile arrest rates of other races.

Note: The annual rape arrest rates for American Indians fluctuate because of the small number of arrests, but the average rate over the period is close to the white rate.

Data source: Analysis of arrest data from the FBI and population data from the U.S. Bureau of the Census. [See arrest rate data source note on page 32 for details.]

In 1999, juvenile arrest rates for robbery fell to their lowest level in more than 20 years

The decline in robbery arrests was interrupted in the late 1980s

The juvenile arrest rate for robbery declined steadily for most of the 1980s. There was, however, an abrupt turnabout in 1989. In the 6 years between 1988 and 1995, the juvenile robbery arrest rate increased 70%, to a level nearly 20% above the 1980 rate. Over this period, the juvenile proportion of robbery arrests increased from 22% to 32%. The decline in the juvenile robbery arrest rate from 1995 to 1999 was even more abrupt. During this 4-year period, the rate was cut in half, falling to a point 20% below the previous low point in 1988.

Arrest rate trends by gender and race parallel the overall pattern

Throughout the 1980s, 7% of all juvenile robbery arrests were arrests of females. This proportion increased to 9% in the 1990s, reflecting the greater percentage increase in the female arrest rate between 1988 and 1995 (109% for females vs. 66% for males). Between 1995 and 1999, rates declined at similar proportions for females and males (52% vs. 56%).

Black juveniles had far higher robbery arrest rates than other juveniles throughout the 1980s and 1990s, although the racial disparity decreased in the late 1990s. The trends in arrest rates within racial groups, however, generally paralleled each other. Whatever caused these large changes in juvenile robbery arrests (and, by inference, juvenile robberies) affected all races equally.

Throughout the 1980s and 1990s, similar trends were found in the robbery arrest rates of juvenile males and females and of each racial group

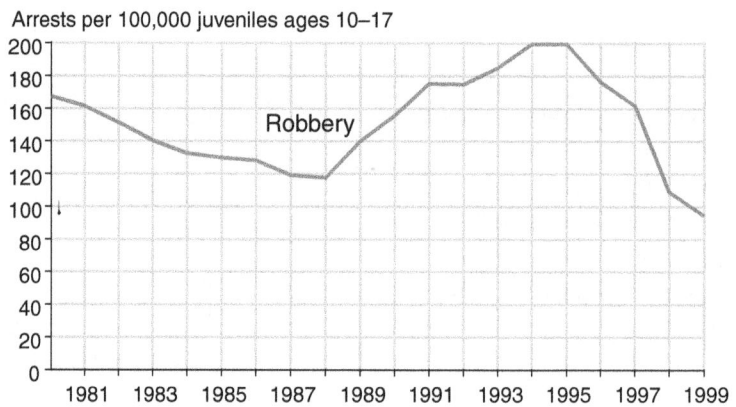

Robbery arrest rate trends by gender and race

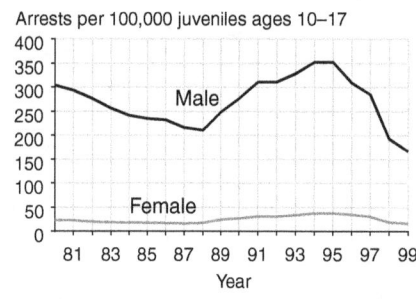

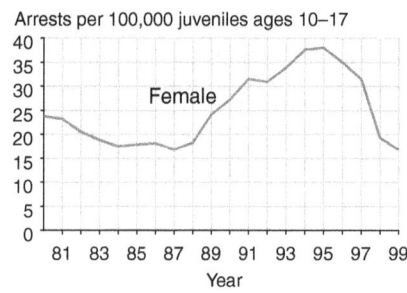

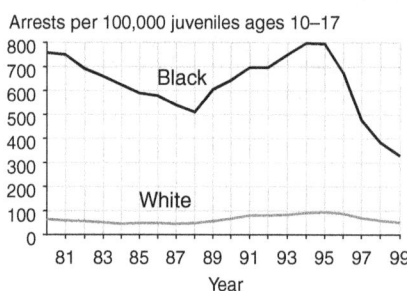

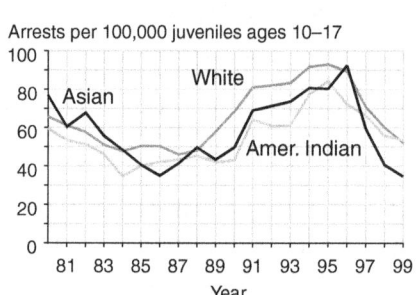

■ In 1980, the black juvenile arrest rate for robbery was 12 times the white rate; by 1999, this ratio had fallen to 6 to 1, reflecting the substantial decline in the black rate in the latter part of the 1990s.

Data source: Analysis of arrest data from the FBI and population data from the U.S. Bureau of the Census. [See arrest rate data source note on page 32 for details.]

Unlike trends for other violent crimes, juvenile arrest rates for aggravated assault remained high in 1999

The 1999 juvenile arrest rate for aggravated assault was above the mid-1980 levels

While the juvenile arrest rates for other violent crimes fell to (or near) their lowest levels in two decades in 1999, the juvenile arrest rate for aggravated assault did not. As with murder and robbery, the juvenile arrest rate for aggravated assault grew substantially between 1987 and 1994 (up 93%, 68%, and 79%, respectively). The murder and robbery rates fell precipitously between 1994 and 1999 (65% and 53%, respectively); however, the aggravated assault arrest rate fell just 24%. The large declines in the murder and robbery arrest rates wiped out all of their increases of the late 1980s and early 1990s, dropping their levels to at least a 20-year low. In contrast, the relatively small decline in the aggravated assault arrest rate left the 1999 rate still 37% above the 1987 level.

Male and black rates declined more than female and white rates

From 1987 to 1999, aggravated assault arrest rates for male and female juveniles rose substantially and then fell. The female rate, however, rose more and then fell far less than the male rate. As a result, in 1999, the female arrest rate was almost double its 1987 level, whereas the male rate was just 25% greater. The arrest rate rose more for whites than blacks between 1987 and 1994 (85% vs. 66%), then fell substantially less for whites. Consequently, in 1999, the black juvenile arrest rate was within 3% of the 1987 rate, but the white rate was 61% greater.

For most years between 1980 and 1999, the juvenile arrest rate for aggravated assault increased—most strikingly for young females

Arrests per 100,000 juveniles ages 10–17

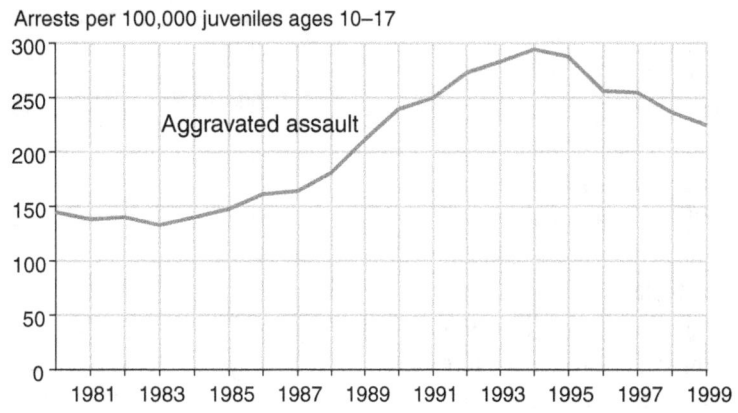

Aggravated assault arrest rate trends by gender and race

Arrests per 100,000 juveniles ages 10–17

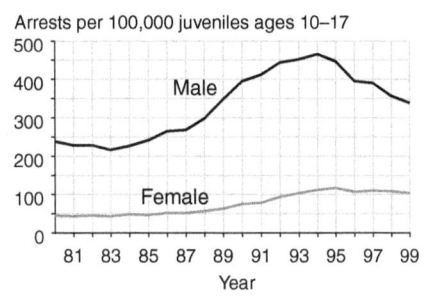

Arrests per 100,000 juveniles ages 10–17

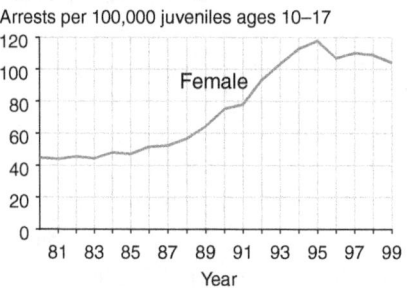

Arrests per 100,000 juveniles ages 10–17

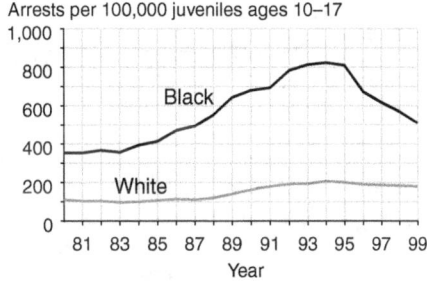

Arrests per 100,000 juveniles ages 10–17

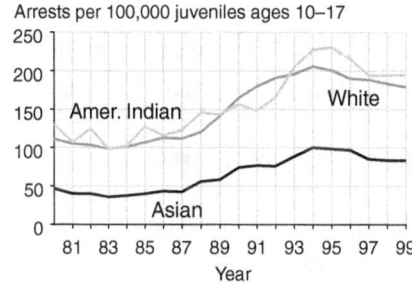

■ The disproportionate increase in female arrest rates for aggravated assault compared with male rates indicates that the rates were affected by factors that impinged differently on females and males. One possible explanation may be found in policy changes over this period that encourage arrests in domestic violence incidents (see discussion on pages 11–12).

Data source: Analysis of arrest data from the FBI and population data from the U.S. Bureau of the Census. [See arrest rate data source note on page 32 for details.]

Juveniles were less likely to be arrested for property crimes in 1999 than they were 20 years earlier

After years of stability, juvenile property crime arrest rates fell in the late 1990s

Between 1980 and 1997, the juvenile arrest rate for Property Crime Index offenses varied little, always remaining within 10% of the average for the period. However, 1998 and 1999 saw significant declines in these arrests. By 1999, the juvenile arrest rate had fallen to a point 28% below the average for 1980–97 and was at its lowest level in at least 20 years. This substantial decline in a high-volume offense category meant that far fewer juveniles charged with property offenses were entering the juvenile justice system.

Female property crime arrest rates increased from 1980 to 1999

In 1980, the juvenile male arrest rate for Property Crime Index offenses was four times the female rate; by 1999, the male rate was just twice the female rate. These two rates converged because the male rate declined 41% over this period while the female rate increased 8%. The stark differences in the male and female trends point to several possibilities, including gender-specific changes in these behaviors and/or an increased willingness to arrest female offenders.

The Property Crime Index arrest rate fell equally for white and black juveniles in the late 1990s, with drops of 35% for blacks and 30% for whites from 1994 to 1999. In the 20 years from 1980 to 1999, the black arrest rate for property crimes remained consistently twice the white rate.

Between 1980 and 1999, the juvenile arrest rate for Property Crime Index offenses fell for all four races and for males, but not for females

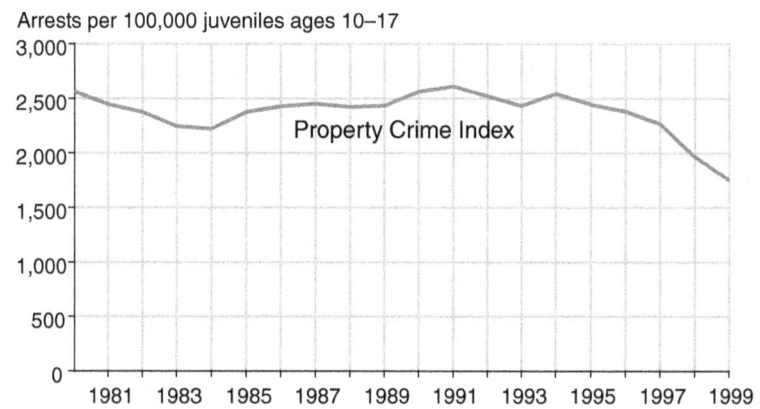

Property Crime Index arrest rate trends by gender and race

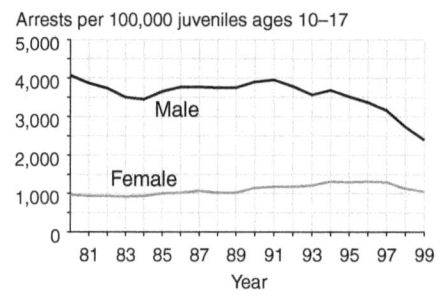
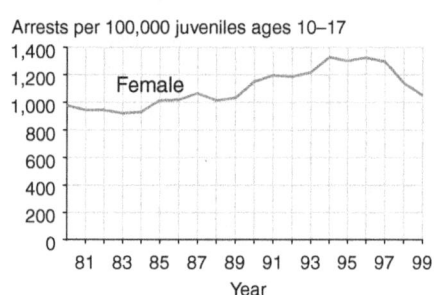
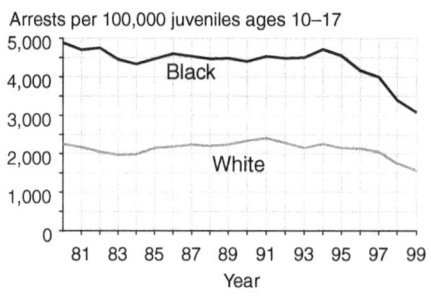
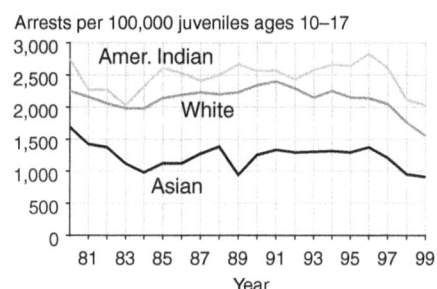

■ The Property Crime Index includes burglary, larceny-theft, motor vehicle theft, and arson. It is dominated by larceny-theft, which in 1999 contributed 70% of all juvenile Property Crime Index arrests. Therefore, the trends in Property Crime Index arrests largely reflect the trends in arrests for larceny-theft.

Data source: Analysis of arrest data from the FBI and population data from the U.S. Bureau of the Census. [See arrest rate data source note on page 32 for details.]

Juvenile arrest rates for burglary declined substantially in the 1980s and 1990s

Juvenile arrests for burglary fell more than adult arrests

In 1980, 45% of all persons arrested for burglary were under age 18. During the 1980s, juvenile burglary arrests fell 43%, while adult arrests dropped just 4%. As a result, in 1989, juveniles were involved in just 32% of all burglary arrests. During the 1990s, burglary arrests dropped one-third for both juveniles and adults. As a result of these declines, juveniles were less than half as likely to be arrested for burglary in 1999 than they were in 1980.

Compared with males, the female arrest rate for burglary remained high

The large decline in the juvenile burglary arrest rate was primarily the result of a decline in male arrests. In 1980, 6% of juveniles arrested for burglary were female; by 1999, 11% were female. Although burglary remained primarily a male behavior in 1999, the substantial decline in the male arrest rate between 1980 and 1999 stands in sharp contrast to the stability of the female rate between 1983 and 1999. Over this period, while the male rate fell 51%, the female rate dropped just 12%.

Racial disparity in juvenile burglary arrest rates has diminished

In 1980, the black juvenile arrest rate for burglary was 2.0 times the white rate; by 1999, the ratio had fallen to 1.7. Thus, during this period, while both rates fell by more than half, the black arrest rate fell more than the white rate (65% vs. 58%).

Unique among major offense categories tracked by the FBI's UCR Program, the juvenile arrest rate for burglary fell 60% between 1980 and 1999

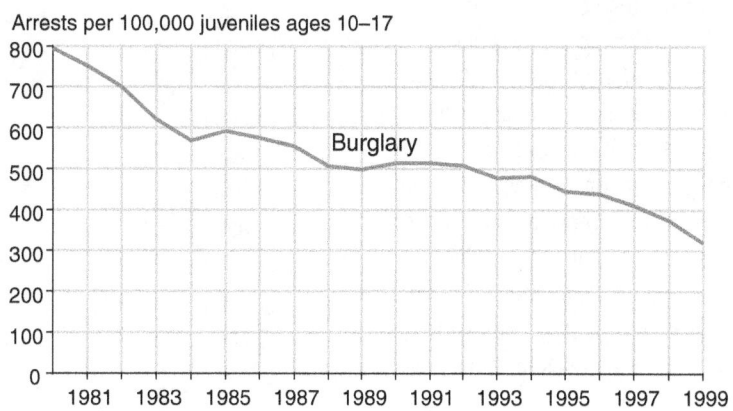

Burglary arrest rate trends by gender and race

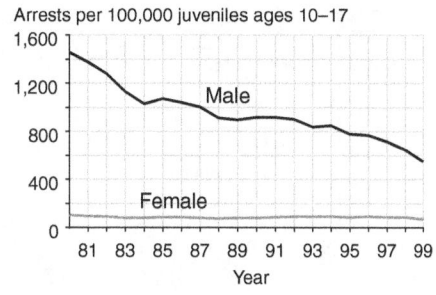
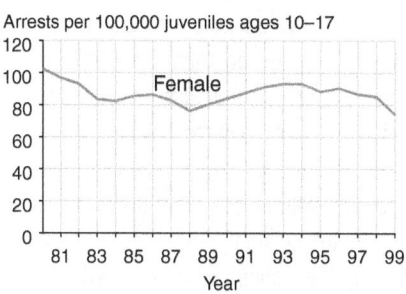

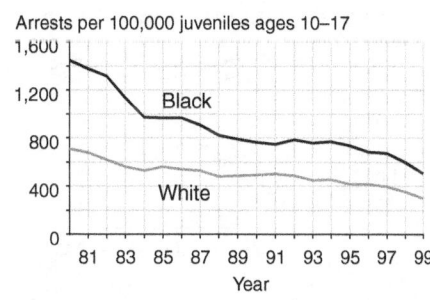
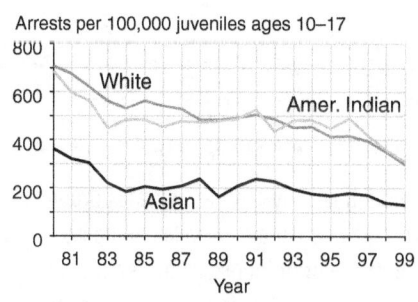

■ In contrast to the declining male trend, the juvenile female arrest rate for burglary was relatively stable over most of the 1980s and 1990s.

Data source: Analysis of arrest data from the FBI and population data from the U.S. Bureau of the Census. [See arrest rate data source note on page 32 for details.]

Juvenile arrest rates for larceny-theft fell in 1999 to a level lower than any since at least 1980

Juvenile larceny-theft rates fell in the late 1990s

Larceny-theft is the unlawful taking of property from the possession of another. This crime group includes such offenses as shoplifting, bicycle theft, and pickpocketing—or thefts without the use of force, threat, or fraud. For juveniles, it has been the most common type of crime: in 1999, one in six juvenile arrests was for larceny-theft. The stability of juvenile arrest rates for larceny-theft over most of the last two decades stands in stark contrast to the large swings in arrest rates for other types of crimes.

Between 1980 and 1997, the annual juvenile arrest rates for larceny-theft stayed within 10% of the average rate for the period. However, in 1998 and again in 1999, the arrest rate dropped outside its traditional levels, falling in 1999 to 22% below the 1980–97 average. This decline in arrests for a high-volume offense translated into a meaningfully smaller number of juveniles entering the justice system charged with property crimes in the late 1990s.

Declines were greater for males than females and blacks than whites

Although larceny-theft arrest rates dropped for male and female juveniles in the late 1990s, the prior increases for females resulted in their 1999 rate being 11% above their 1980 rate, whereas the 1999 rate for males was 29% below their 1980 rate. From 1980 to 1999, the ratio of black-to-white arrest rates dropped from 2.3 to 1.9, reflecting a greater decline in the black rate than in the white rate (30% vs. 16% decline).

In contrast to the other major property crimes of burglary and motor vehicle theft, the annual rates of juvenile arrests for larceny-theft were relatively stable over most of the 1980s and 1990s

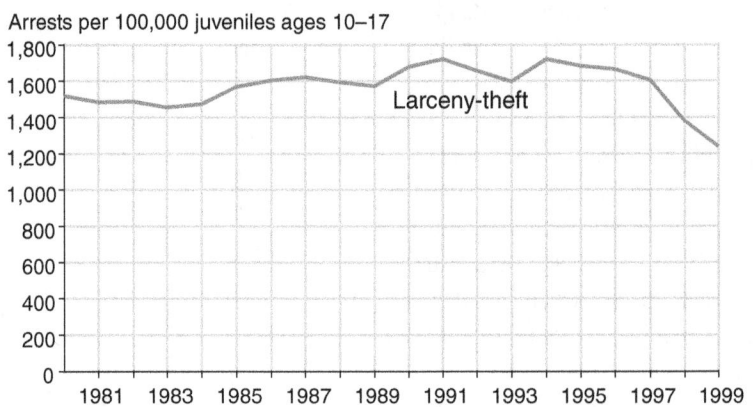

Larceny-theft arrest rate trends by gender and race

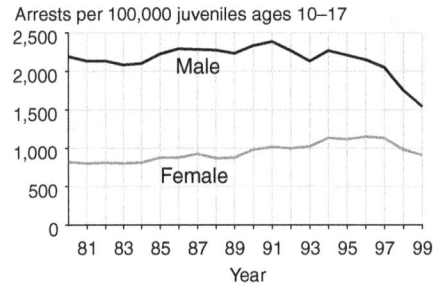

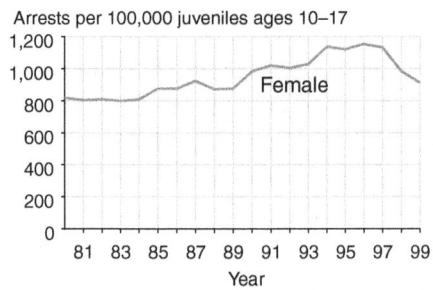

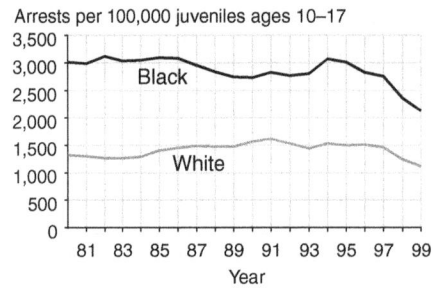

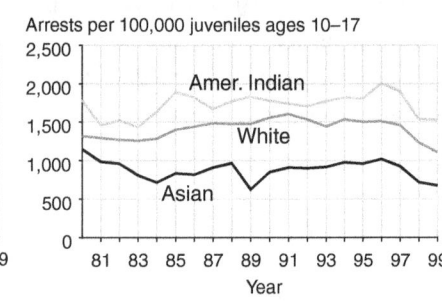

- In the 1990s, the juvenile male arrest rate for larceny-theft fell, while the female rate grew and then fell to the levels observed at the beginning of the decade.

- The black rate declined more than the white rate in the 1990s.

Data source: Analysis of arrest data from the FBI and population data from the U.S. Bureau of the Census. [See arrest rate data source note on page 32 for details.]

The growth in juvenile motor vehicle theft arrest rates that began in 1984 was erased by 1999

Juvenile arrest rates for motor vehicle theft soared in the 1980s

Juvenile arrest rates for motor vehicle theft fell to a low point in 1983 for males and females and for whites, blacks, and American Indians. (The Asian rate bottomed out in 1984.) After 1983, and predating the growth in juvenile arrests for violent crime, the juvenile arrest rate for motor vehicle theft increased each year through 1990, when the rate was 138% above its 1983 level. In contrast, the juvenile arrest rate for motor vehicle theft fell in the 1990s—by 1999, it was near its 1983 low.

The juvenile arrest rate trends for motor vehicle theft differed from those for the other high-volume theft crimes of burglary and larceny-theft. In the 1980s and 1990s, the burglary arrest rate declined consistently and the larceny-theft rate remained relatively stable, but the motor vehicle theft rate soared and then dropped just as dramatically.

Male and female juvenile arrest rates for motor vehicle theft displayed generally similar trends in the 1980s and 1990s, first increasing then decreasing. However, the male rate peaked in 1990, whereas the female rate did not peak until 1993. With a longer period of decline than the female rate, the male rate in 1999 fell to within 7% of its 1983 low, while the female rate was still 76% above its low point.

The motor vehicle theft arrest rate for black juveniles grew far more than the rate for whites between 1983 and 1989 (254% vs. 86%). By 1999, the white rate had returned to its 1983 low, but the black rate was 58% greater than its 1983 level.

The juvenile arrest rate for motor vehicle theft in 1999 was half that at the beginning of the decade

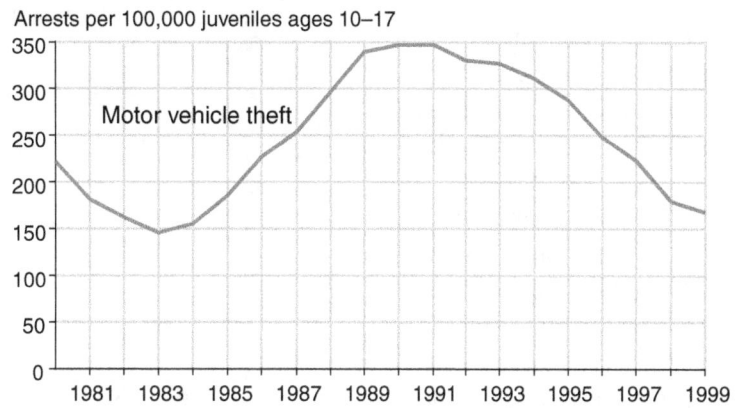

Motor vehicle theft arrest rate trends by gender and race

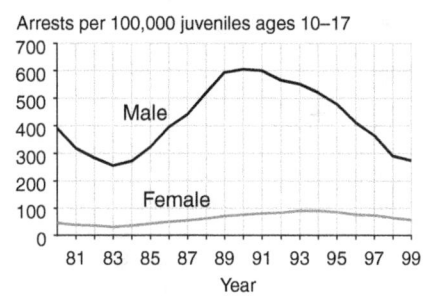

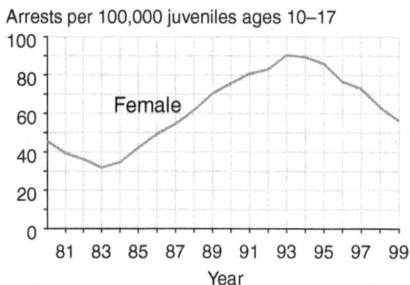

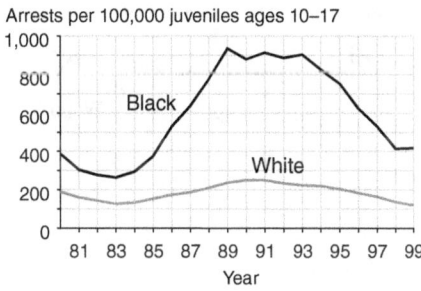

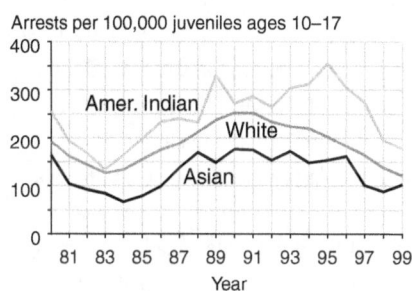

- ■ Although both the male and female arrest rates for motor vehicle theft peaked and then declined between 1980 and 1999, the male peak preceded the female peak by 3 years (1990 vs. 1993).

- ■ The relative growth and subsequent decline in the motor vehicle theft arrest rate was far more pronounced for black juveniles than white juveniles.

Data source: Analysis of arrest data from the FBI and population data from the U.S. Bureau of the Census. [See arrest rate data source note on page 32 for detail.]

More than half of all persons arrested for arson in 1999 were under age 18, and 1 in 5 was under 13

Arson is the criminal act with the largest proportion of juvenile arrestees

In 1999, 54% of all persons arrested for arson were juveniles. Arson is also the criminal act with the largest percentage of arrestees under the age of 13 (19%). In comparison, 31% of all larceny-theft arrests in 1999 involved juveniles, and 4% involved juveniles under age 13. Young persons are brought into the juvenile justice system in such high proportions for the crime of arson in part because arson is commonly considered an indicator of serious emotional problems in youth.

The juvenile arrest rate for arson grew 56% from 1987 to 1994, then fell

The pattern of stability, growth, and decline in the juvenile arrest rate for arson in the 1980s and 1990s was similar in magnitude and character to the trend in juvenile violent crime arrest rates. After years of stability, the rate increased more than 50% before falling and returning by 1999 to a level similar to that before the increase. During the period of increase, the female rate increased more than the male rate. During the period of decline, the male and female rates declined proportionally. However, because of the greater increase in the female rate, these declines left the female rate in 1999 about 30% above its level in the early 1980s, while the male rate was just 15% above its early 1980s levels. One major distinction between violent crime and arson arrest rates over this period was that white and black rates were similar for arson but not for violent crime (see page 13).

During the 1990s, the juvenile arrest rate for arson grew substantially and then declined, resulting in a 1999 rate equal to the 1990 rate

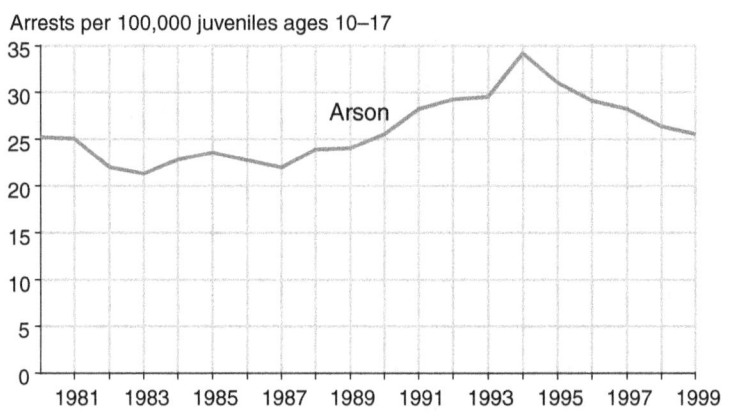
Arrests per 100,000 juveniles ages 10–17

Arson arrest rate trends by gender and race

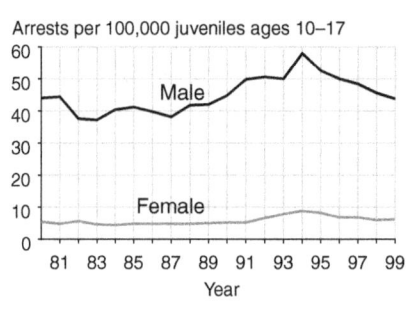
Arrests per 100,000 juveniles ages 10–17

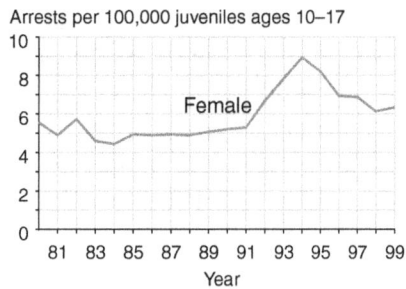
Arrests per 100,000 juveniles ages 10–17

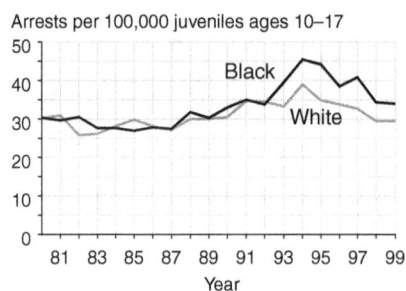
Arrests per 100,000 juveniles ages 10–17

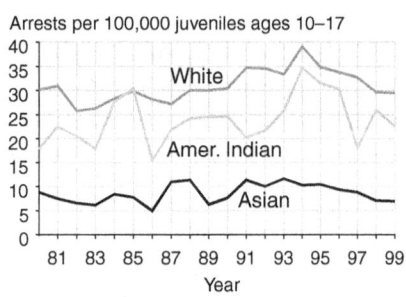
Arrests per 100,000 juveniles ages 10–17

■ From 1980 through 1992, white and black juvenile arrest rates for arson were equal. After 1992, the black rate rose above the white rate.

■ The female juvenile arrest rate for arson increased abruptly between 1991 and 1994.

Data source: Analysis of arrest data from the FBI and population data from the U.S. Bureau of the Census. [See arrest rate data source note on page 32 for details.]

Juvenile arrest rates for simple assault grew substantially through the 1980s and 1990s

Simple assault is the most common of all crimes against persons

In 1999, there were nearly five juvenile arrests for simple assault for every one juvenile arrest for aggravated assault. In contrast to aggravated assault, a simple assault does not involve the use of a weapon and does not result in serious bodily harm to the victim. The lesser severity of simple assault makes the reporting of it to law enforcement less likely and gives law enforcement more discretion in how to handle the incident.

The simple assault arrest rate increased 150% between 1980 and 1999

Unlike most violent crime arrest rates that rose and then fell during the 1980s and 1990s, the juvenile arrest rate for simple assault rose almost continuously from 1983 through 1996 and then maintained this high level through 1999. The large increase in the juvenile rate was paralleled by a similar increase in the adult rate, so that the juvenile proportion of all simple assault arrests was 18% in both 1980 and 1999. As with aggravated assault, the increase in the juvenile female arrest rate for simple assault over the 20-year period far outpaced the increase in the male rate (270% vs. 120%). As a result, between 1980 and 1999, the female proportion of juvenile arrests for simple assault grew from 21% to 30%. From 1980 to 1999, simple assault arrest rates increased substantially for white (160%), black (133%), and American Indian (185%) youth, with rates for Asian youth also increasing but to a smaller degree (39%).

Between 1980 and 1999, simple assault arrest rates for female, male, white, black, and American Indian juveniles more than doubled

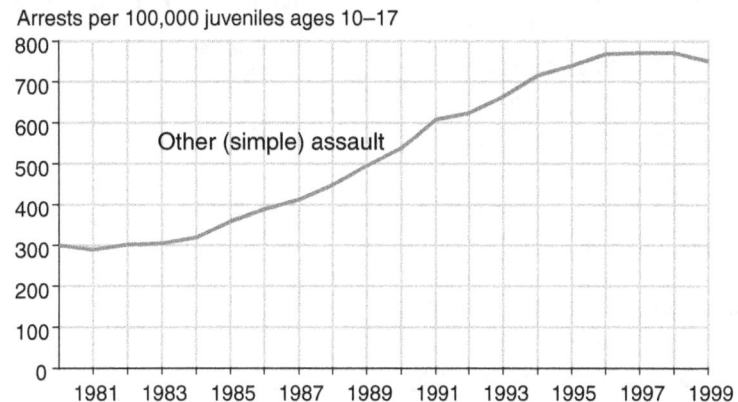

Arrests per 100,000 juveniles ages 10–17

Other (simple) assault arrest rate trends by gender and race

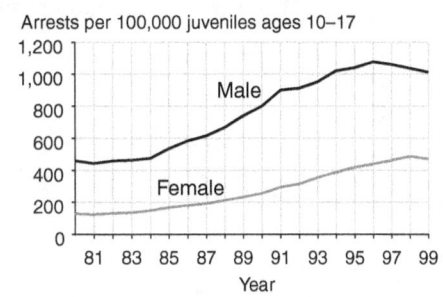

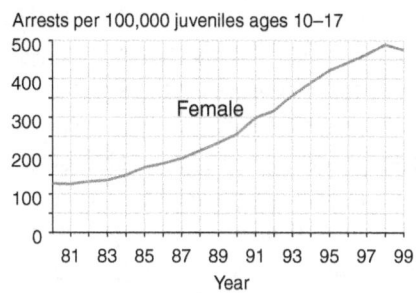

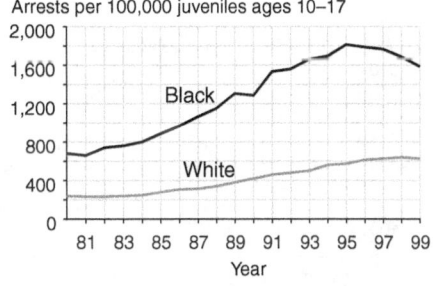

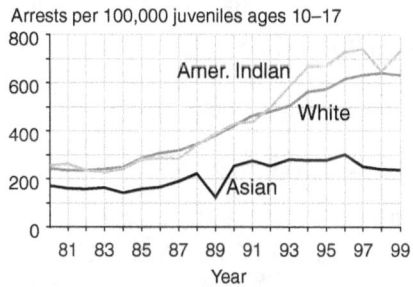

■ In 1999, the ratio of simple to aggravated assault arrests of juveniles varied among gender and racial groups: male (3.0 to 1), female (4.6 to 1), white (3.5 to 1), black (3.1 to 1), American Indian (3.8 to 1), and Asian (2.8 to 1).

Data source: Analysis of arrest data from the FBI and population data from the U.S. Bureau of the Census. [See arrest rate data source note on page 32 for details.]

Juvenile arrest rate trends for weapons law violations have paralleled trends for violent crimes

Juvenile weapons arrest rates peaked in 1993

The juvenile arrest rate for weapons law violations doubled between 1987 and 1993. In 1993, if it is assumed that each arrest involved a different youth, then about 1 of every 500 juveniles ages 10–17 in the population was arrested for at least 1 crime in which the most serious charge was a weapons offense.

Other, more serious crimes also involved the use of a firearm; however, the FBI's arrest statistics classified these arrests by their most serious charge. An analysis of 1997 and 1998 data from the FBI's National Incident-Based Reporting System finds that a firearm was present in 14% of aggravated assaults and 28% of robberies committed by juveniles. If these proportions are applied to the juvenile arrest rates for robbery and aggravated assault, and if again it is assumed that each juvenile is arrested just once in the year, then about 1 of every 300 juveniles ages 10–17 (or 0.3%) was arrested for a weapons-involved crime in 1993. In 1999, the ratio was 1 in 450 (0.2%).

Weapons arrests fell substantially after 1993

The juvenile arrest rate for weapons law violations dropped 38% between 1993 and 1999, to the lowest level in the 1990s. Declines occurred in the rates for males, females, and each racial group. The 1999 rates, however, were all still far above their 1980 levels, with increases as follows: all juveniles (49%), male (43%), female (152%), white (53%), black (50%), American Indian (43%), and Asian (21%).

From the mid-1980s to the mid-1990s, the juvenile arrest rate for weapons law violations increased substantially in all segments of the juvenile population

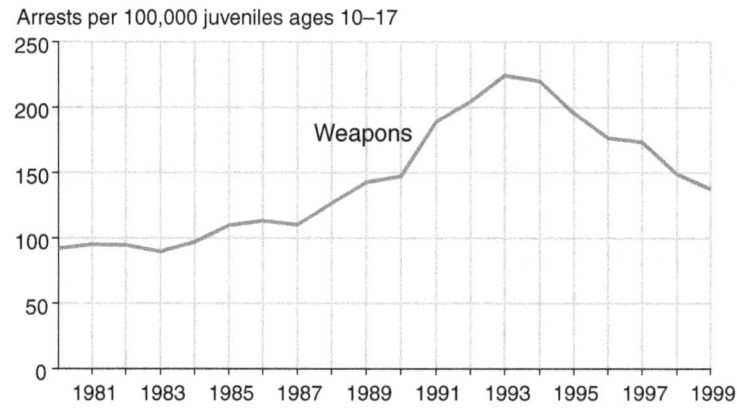

Weapons law violation arrest rate trends by gender and race

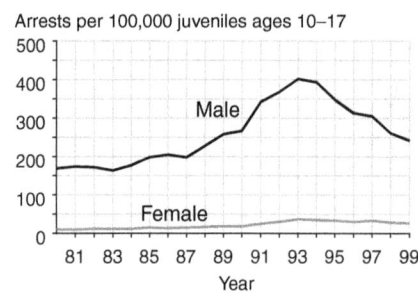

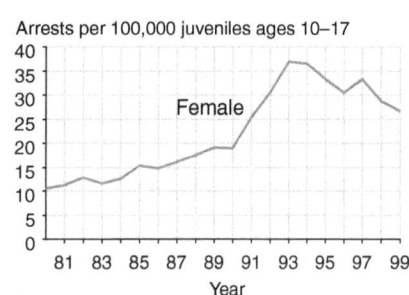

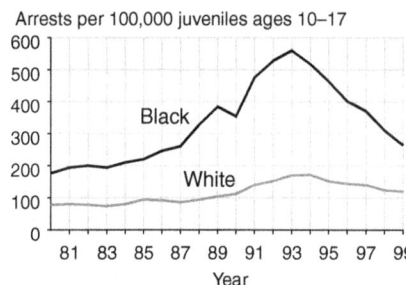

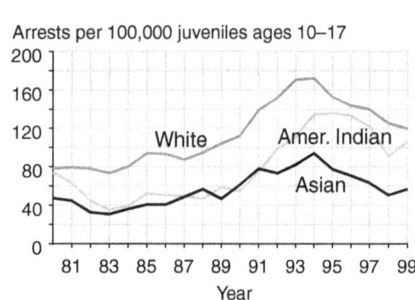

■ Between 1980 and the peak year of 1993, the juvenile arrest rate for weapons law violations increased more for blacks (219%) than for whites (118%), Asians (73%), or American Indians (50%)—and more for females (248%) than males (137%).

Data source: Analysis of arrest data from the FBI and population data from the U.S. Bureau of the Census. [See arrest rate data source note on page 32 for details.]

After more than a decade of relative stability, juvenile drug arrest rates climbed 118% in 5 years

The 1980s saw increased racial disparity in drug arrest rates

The annual juvenile arrest rates for drug abuse violations (a category that includes both drug possession and drug sale) varied within a limited range in the 1980s, staying within 20% of the average for the decade. This general consistency in drug arrest rates contrasts with the large decline in self-reported use of marijuana and other illicit drugs during the decade.

A closer look at juvenile drug arrest rates finds sharp racial differences in the 1980s. The white rate fell 32% over the period, compared with a 249% increase for blacks. In 1980, the white and black arrest rates were essentially equal, with black youth involved in 15% of all juvenile drug arrests. By 1989, the black rate was five times the white rate, and black youth were involved in 49% of all juvenile drug arrests.

Drug arrests soared for all youth between 1992 and 1997

In contrast to the 1980s, the overall juvenile drug arrest rate more than doubled (118%) in the short period between 1992 and 1997. Increases were seen in the rates for all subgroups: male (112%), female (176%), white (187%), American Indian (289%), and Asian (136%). Even the black rate, which had increased dramatically in the 1980s, increased an additional 41% between 1992 and 1997. Between 1997 and 1999, the juvenile drug arrest rate fell marginally, with most of the overall decline attributable to a drop in arrests of black males.

The surge in the juvenile arrest rate for drug abuse violations began years after similar upturns in violent crime and weapons arrests

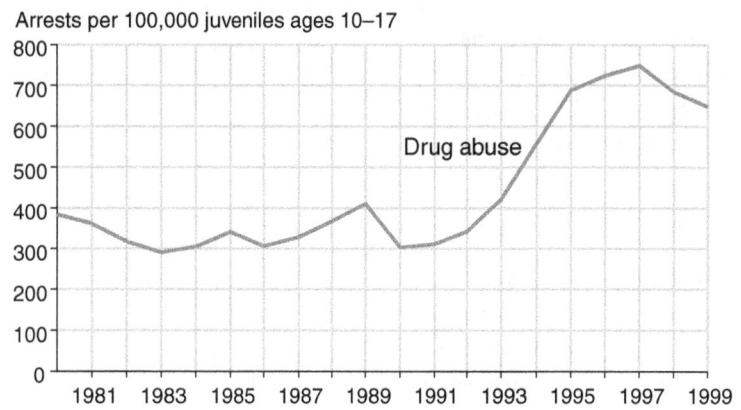

Arrests per 100,000 juveniles ages 10–17

Drug abuse violation arrest rate trends by gender and race

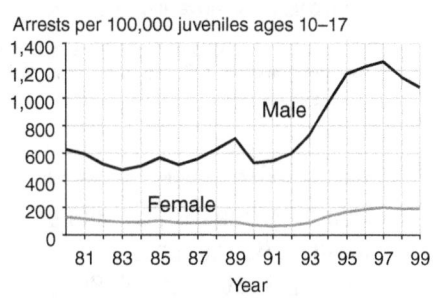

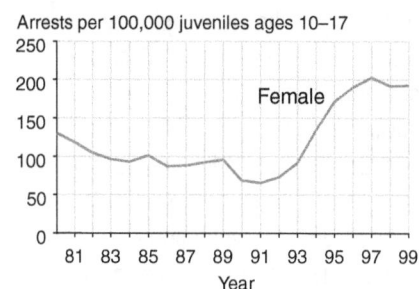

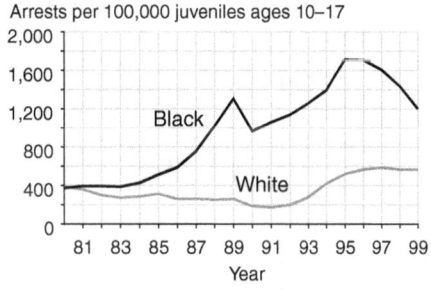

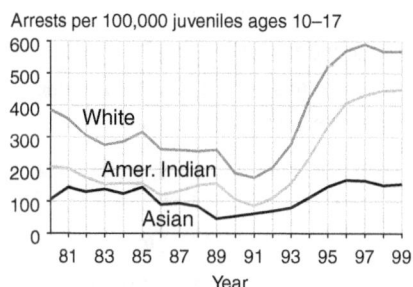

■ The trend in juvenile arrests for drug abuse violations among blacks was different from the trends for other racial groups. While the arrest rate for other races generally declined throughout the 1980s, the rate for black juveniles increased substantially during this period.

Data source: Analysis of arrest data from the FBI and population data from the U.S. Bureau of the Census. [See arrest rate data source note on page 32 for details.]

Clearance proportions give insight into the relative involvement of juveniles and adults in crime

Law enforcement tracks the percentage of reported crimes cleared

The FBI data monitor the proportion of cleared crimes that are cleared by the arrest of only juveniles. This proportion, however, provides only a rough estimate of the percentage of known crimes that were committed by juveniles.

As discussed earlier (see pages 3–4), a crime cleared by the arrest of a juvenile and the arrest of an adult is classified by the FBI as an adult clearance. This means that some cleared crimes with juvenile offenders are not counted in the proportion of crimes cleared by juvenile arrest—a factor that makes the juvenile clearance proportion an underestimate of juvenile involvement in cleared crimes. Research shows, however, that juvenile crimes are more likely than adult crimes to be cleared—a factor that artificially inflates the juvenile clearance proportions. Thus, although the magnitude of the annual proportions of crimes cleared by juvenile arrest may be inaccurate, the trends in these proportions are reasonable indicators of changes in the relative involvement of juveniles in various crimes.

Between 1980 and 1999, the juvenile proportion of Violent Crime Index clearances increased

In the 1980s, between 8% and 11% of all violent crimes cleared by law enforcement were cleared by juvenile arrest. In the 1990s, juvenile involvement ranged between 11% and 14%. This growth in juvenile involvement was reflected in the

Clearance data for 1999 indicate that if all juvenile violent crime ceased, the overall violent crime rate would fall 12%

Percent of crimes cleared by juvenile arrests

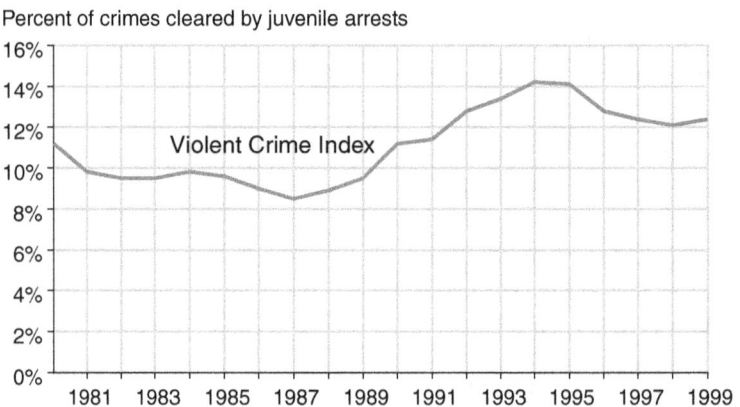

■ Clearance data indicate that juvenile responsibility for violent crime peaked in 1994, when an estimated 14% of all violent crimes cleared by law enforcement involved only juvenile offenders.

Data source: Analysis of the FBI's *Crime in the United States* reports for the years 1980 through 1999 (Washington, DC: U.S. Government Printing Office, 1981 through 2000, respectively).

Data on crimes known and cleared by law enforcement indicate that the juvenile responsibility for property crime was relatively stable over the 1980s and 1990s

Percent of crimes cleared by juvenile arrests

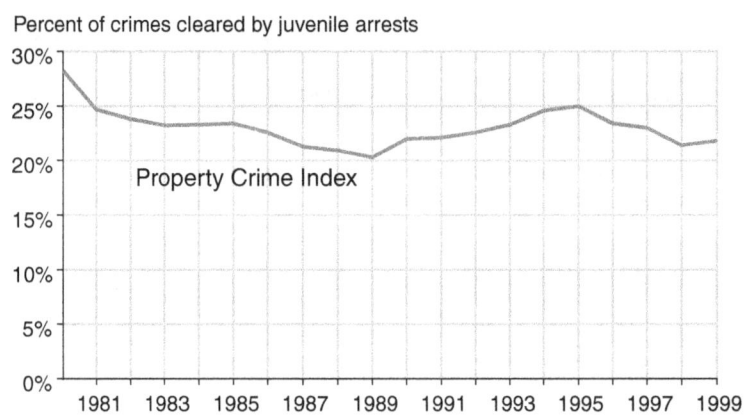

■ Over the period, 1 in every 4 to 5 property crimes cleared by law enforcement was cleared by the arrest of a juvenile.

Data source: Analysis of the FBI's *Crime in the United States* reports for the years 1980 through 1999 (Washington, DC: U.S. Government Printing Office, 1981 through 2000, respectively).

Clearance statistics indicate that juvenile responsibility for each of the violent offenses peaked in the mid-1990s and then fell

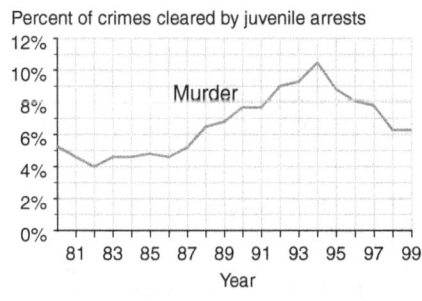

Percent of crimes cleared by juvenile arrests

Murder

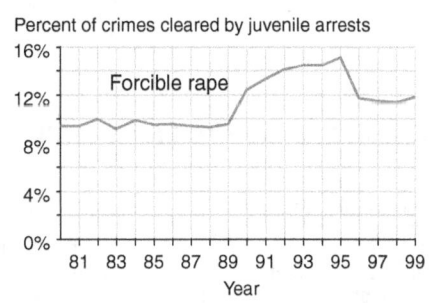

Percent of crimes cleared by juvenile arrests

Forcible rape

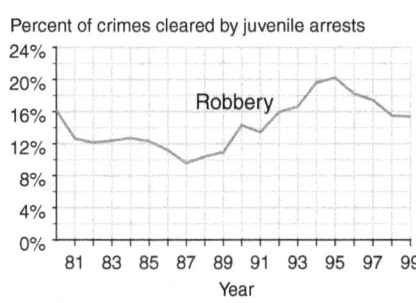

Percent of crimes cleared by juvenile arrests

Robbery

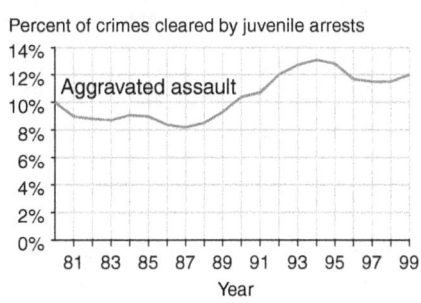

Percent of crimes cleared by juvenile arrests

Aggravated assault

Clearance data indicate that juvenile responsibility for burglary, larceny-theft, and motor vehicle theft was less in 1999 than in 1980

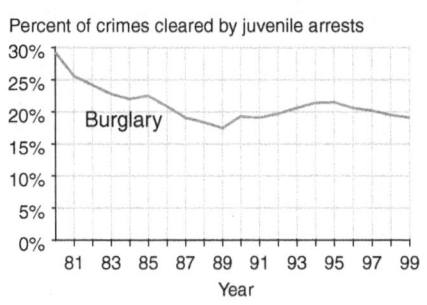

Percent of crimes cleared by juvenile arrests

Burglary

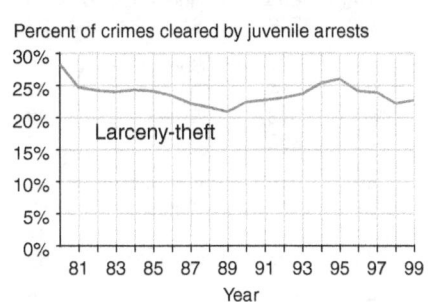

Percent of crimes cleared by juvenile arrests

Larceny-theft

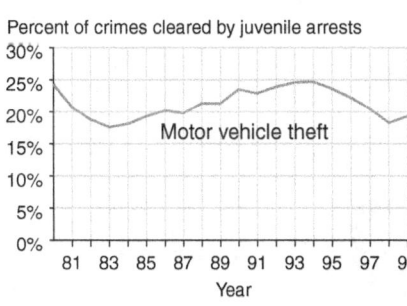

Percent of crimes cleared by juvenile arrests

Motor vehicle theft

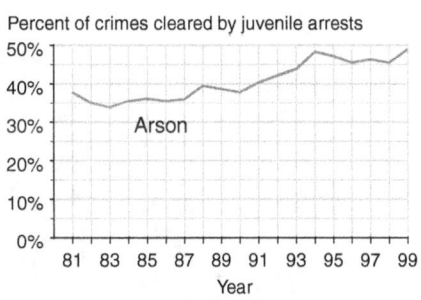

Percent of crimes cleared by juvenile arrests

Arson

Note: Arson clearance data were first reported in 1981.

Data source: Analysis of the FBI's *Crime in the United States* reports for the years 1980 through 1999 (Washington, DC: U.S. Government Printing Office, 1981 through 2000, respectively).

greater increase in violent crime arrests for juveniles (67%) than for adults (31%) between 1986 and 1995.

Each of the four Violent Crime Index offenses showed an increase in the juvenile proportion of crimes cleared. The most notable growth was in murder clearances. From the early 1980s to 1994, the proportion of murders cleared by juvenile arrests grew from less than 5% to more than 10%. The juvenile involvement in murder, however, was less than in other violent crimes. The juvenile proportion of clearances also reached peak levels during the mid-1990s for other Violent Crime Index offenses: forcible rape in 1995 (15%), robbery in 1995 (20%), and aggravated assault in 1994 (13%). Between the mid-1990s and 1999, the juvenile proportion of clearances fell to 12% for forcible rape and to 15% for robbery. In contrast, the juvenile proportion of aggravated assault clearances changed little after the mid-1990s.

The juvenile proportion of Property Crime Index clearances fell throughout the 1980s

In the 1980s, the juvenile proportion of cleared Property Crime Index offenses dropped from 28% to 20%. Although there was an increase in the 1990s, the juvenile proportion ended the decade at the level at which it began (22%). The crimes of burglary, larceny-theft, and motor vehicle theft all ended this 20-year period with juvenile clearance proportions near their lows for the period (19%, 23%, and 19%, respectively). Only the crime of arson ended the period with a substantially higher proportion of crimes cleared by juvenile arrest. For arson, the juvenile proportion of clearances grew from 35% in the early 1980s to 49% in 1999.

In 1999, about two-thirds of the States had a juvenile violent crime arrest rate below the national average

States with the lowest reported juvenile violent crime arrest rates in 1999 were Vermont, North Dakota, West Virginia, Nebraska, and New Hampshire

State	Reporting population coverage	Violent Crime Index	Murder	Forcible rape	Robbery	Agg. assault	State	Reporting population coverage	Violent Crime Index	Murder	Forcible rape	Robbery	Agg. assault
		Arrests per 100,000 juveniles ages 10–17							Arrests per 100,000 juveniles ages 10–17				
United States	**69%**	**366**	**5**	**17**	**99**	**246**	Missouri	58%	312	7	18	102	186
Alabama	93	148	4	4	57	83	Montana	49	315	11	22	58	224
Alaska	90	279	6	27	58	188	Nebraska	92	119	2	10	46	61
Arizona	92	316	5	6	55	250	Nevada	97	288	6	15	126	142
Arkansas	95	228	6	15	49	158	New Hampshire	39	124	0	5	57	62
California	100	498	5	11	154	328	New Jersey	96	409	2	12	146	249
Colorado	62	300	7	48	55	190	New Mexico	57	357	6	15	33	304
Connecticut	95	339	2	16	82	239	New York	32	336	3	8	116	209
Delaware	100	766	0	91	185	490	North Carolina	88	334	7	8	85	234
Dist. of Columbia	0	NA	NA	NA	NA	NA	North Dakota	74	92	2	9	12	70
Florida	100	672	5	23	164	479	Ohio	53	248	1	31	68	148
Georgia	31	188	5	13	40	129	Oklahoma	0	NA	NA	NA	NA	NA
Hawaii	88	220	2	13	96	108	Oregon	94	203	3	11	58	131
Idaho	86	196	0	14	13	169	Pennsylvania	77	422	4	20	133	265
Illinois	23	1,058	28	56	374	600	Rhode Island	100	246	4	17	85	140
Indiana	58	393	8	8	68	309	South Carolina	23	400	5	27	91	277
Iowa	81	267	1	13	31	222	South Dakota	71	167	1	16	21	128
Kansas	0	NA	NA	NA	NA	NA	Tennessee	51	250	7	7	52	184
Kentucky	11	516	8	8	107	393	Texas	90	235	5	18	62	150
Louisiana	75	461	7	20	68	366	Utah	68	253	1	15	27	209
Maine	0	NA	NA	NA	NA	NA	Vermont	81	60	0	18	0	42
Maryland	60	304	2	11	88	203	Virginia	68	191	4	7	59	120
Massachusetts	78	454	1	11	79	363	Washington	74	335	3	30	81	220
Michigan	82	195	6	19	44	127	West Virginia	52	95	0	2	17	76
Minnesota	85	275	1	30	65	179	Wisconsin	0	NA	NA	NA	NA	NA
Mississippi	40	189	8	23	72	86	Wyoming	98	146	0	8	13	125

NA = Arrest counts were not available for this State in the FBI's *Crime in the United States 1999*.

Notes: Arrest rates for jurisdictions with less than complete reporting may not be representative of the entire State. In the map, rates were classified as "Data not available" when agencies with jurisdiction over more than 50% of their State's population did not report. Readers should consult the related technical note on page 32. Detail may not add to totals because of rounding.

Data source: Analysis of arrest data from the FBI's *Crime in the United States 1999* and population data from the U.S. Bureau of the Census' *Estimates of the population of States by age, sex, race, and Hispanic origin: 1999* [machine-readable data file].

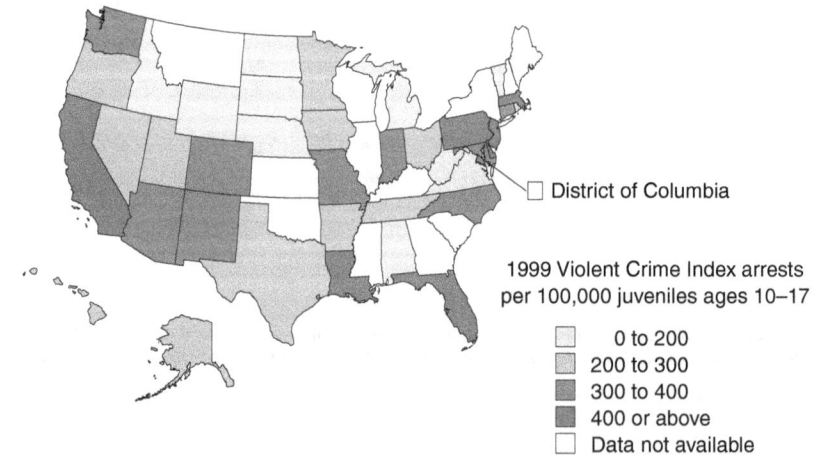

District of Columbia

1999 Violent Crime Index arrests per 100,000 juveniles ages 10–17

- 0 to 200
- 200 to 300
- 300 to 400
- 400 or above
- Data not available

High violent crime arrest rates are found in a relatively small proportion of counties

In 1998, the national juvenile arrest rate for offenses included in the Violent Crime Index was 394 arrests of persons under age 18 for every 100,000 persons ages 10–17 in the U.S. population. Just 10% of the 3,141 counties in the U.S. reported a juvenile violent crime arrest rate higher

than the national average. The highest rate reported by a county was more than four times the national rate. Six in ten reporting counties had rates less than half the national average. Half of all reporting counties had juvenile violent crime arrest rates less than 137, and nearly one-fourth

reported no violent crime arrests at all for the year. However, the fact that high rates of juvenile violent crime arrests are found in counties with small populations and in counties with large populations indicates that high levels of juvenile violence can occur in any community.

Juvenile violent crime arrest rates varied considerably among counties within a State in 1998

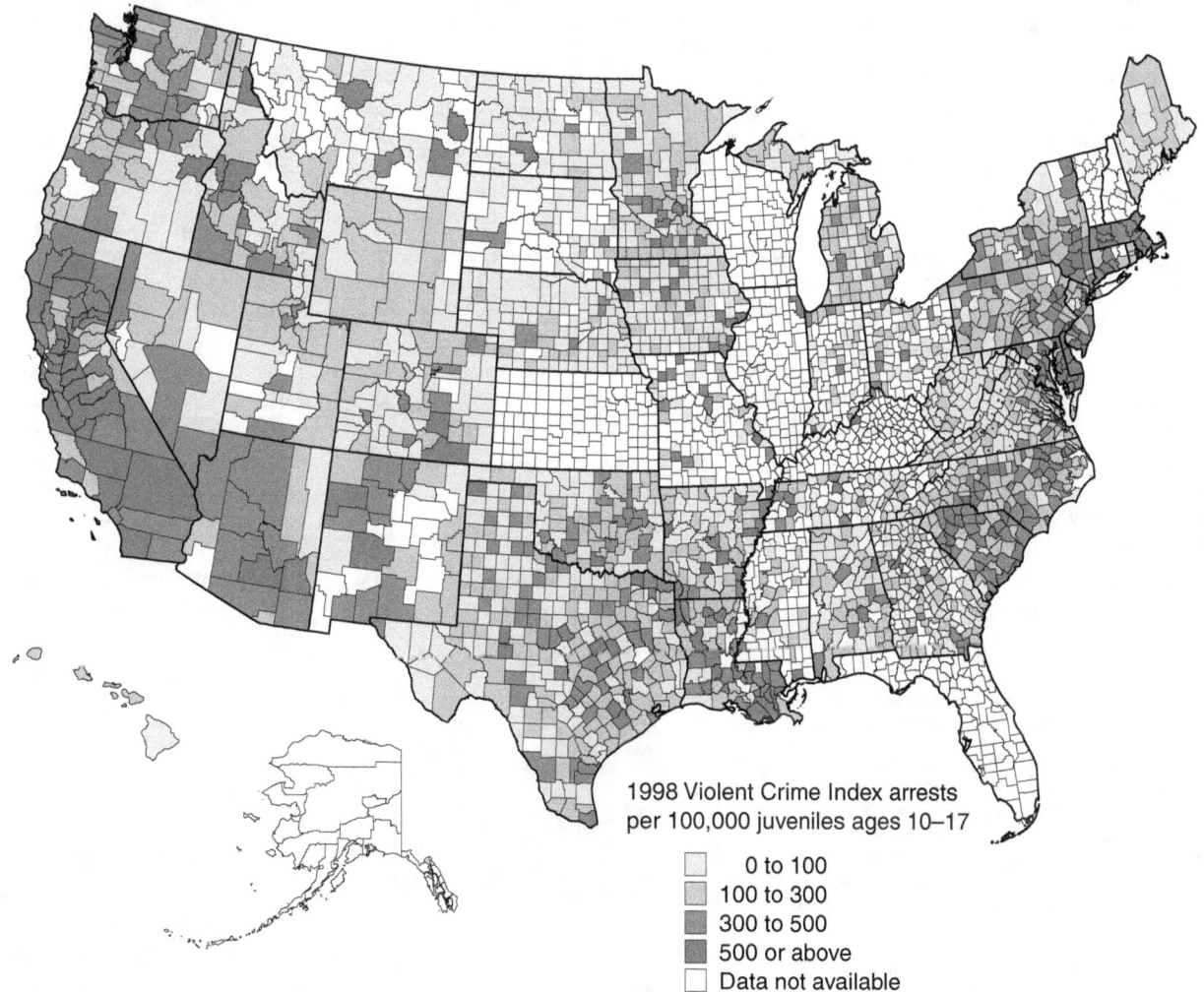

1998 Violent Crime Index arrests
per 100,000 juveniles ages 10–17

- 0 to 100
- 100 to 300
- 300 to 500
- 500 or above
- Data not available

Note: Rates were classified as "Data not available" when agencies with jurisdiction over more than 50% of their county's population did not report.

Data source: Analysis of arrest estimates from the Inter-university Consortium for Political and Social Research's *Uniform Crime Reporting Program data [United States]: County-level detailed arrest and offense data, 1998* [machine-readable data file] and population estimates from the U.S. Bureau of the Census' *Estimates of the population of counties by age and sex: 1990–1999* [machine-readable data files available online, released August 30, 2000].

States with high juvenile property crime arrest rates in 1999 tended to have low violent crime arrest rates

The populous States of California, Michigan, New Jersey, New York, Pennsylvania, Ohio, Texas, and Virginia reported juvenile Property Crime Index arrest rates below the national average in 1999

State	Reporting population coverage	Arrests per 100,000 juveniles ages 10–17 Property Crime Index	Burglary	Larceny-theft	Motor vehicle theft	Arson	State	Reporting population coverage	Arrests per 100,000 juveniles ages 10–17 Property Crime Index	Burglary	Larceny-theft	Motor vehicle theft	Arson
United States	**69%**	**1,844**	**348**	**1,291**	**177**	**28**	Missouri	58%	2,273	314	1,665	258	37
Alabama	93	932	155	728	47	3	Montana	49	3,496	248	3,013	204	31
Alaska	90	2,302	415	1,644	233	11	Nebraska	92	2,716	254	2,269	130	63
Arizona	92	2,334	352	1,738	212	32	Nevada	97	2,526	524	1,709	257	37
Arkansas	95	1,573	317	1,185	64	8	New Hampshire	39	1,262	147	1,010	67	37
California	100	1,643	462	971	180	30	New Jersey	96	1,417	230	1,082	61	43
Colorado	62	2,874	314	2,249	263	49	New Mexico	57	1,973	217	1,664	82	9
Connecticut	95	1,445	223	1,069	136	17	New York	32	1,745	373	1,240	105	28
Delaware	100	2,002	423	1,418	120	41	North Carolina	88	1,717	411	1,190	86	29
Dist. of Columbia	0	NA	NA	NA	NA	NA	North Dakota	74	2,154	292	1,578	272	12
Florida	100	2,713	643	1,756	294	19	Ohio	53	1,509	263	1,073	129	45
Georgia	31	1,603	319	1,170	98	15	Oklahoma	0	NA	NA	NA	NA	NA
Hawaii	88	2,076	338	1,513	216	9	Oregon	94	2,531	339	1,945	185	61
Idaho	86	2,546	365	1,999	144	38	Pennsylvania	77	1,425	251	921	216	37
Illinois	23	2,637	408	884	1,315	30	Rhode Island	100	1,570	298	1,029	210	33
Indiana	58	1,705	195	1,329	162	18	South Carolina	23	2,113	294	1,693	95	31
Iowa	81	1,998	261	1,603	104	31	South Dakota	71	2,375	359	1,871	100	46
Kansas	0	NA	NA	NA	NA	NA	Tennessee	51	1,804	186	1,503	96	19
Kentucky	11	2,291	411	1,473	363	44	Texas	90	1,682	296	1,232	137	16
Louisiana	75	2,381	527	1,725	101	28	Utah	68	2,675	229	2,243	164	39
Maine	0	NA	NA	NA	NA	NA	Vermont	81	796	211	515	64	7
Maryland	60	1,982	374	1,403	148	56	Virginia	68	1,469	229	1,060	142	38
Massachusetts	78	734	171	474	77	12	Washington	74	3,073	480	2,331	216	45
Michigan	82	1,108	158	845	87	18	West Virginia	52	999	137	756	95	11
Minnesota	85	2,381	266	1,825	255	34	Wisconsin	0	NA	NA	NA	NA	NA
Mississippi	40	2,095	466	1,484	130	15	Wyoming	98	2,455	224	2,108	117	6

NA = Arrest counts were not available for this State in the FBI's *Crime in the United States 1999*.

Notes: Arrest rates for jurisdictions with less than complete reporting may not be representative of the entire State. In the map, rates were classified as "Data not available" when agencies with jurisdiction over more than 50% of their State's population did not report. Readers should consult the related technical note on page 32. Detail may not add to totals because of rounding.

Data source: Analysis of arrest data from the FBI's *Crime in the United States 1999* and population data from the Bureau of the Census' *Estimates of the population of States by age, sex, race, and Hispanic origin: 1999* [machine-readable data file].

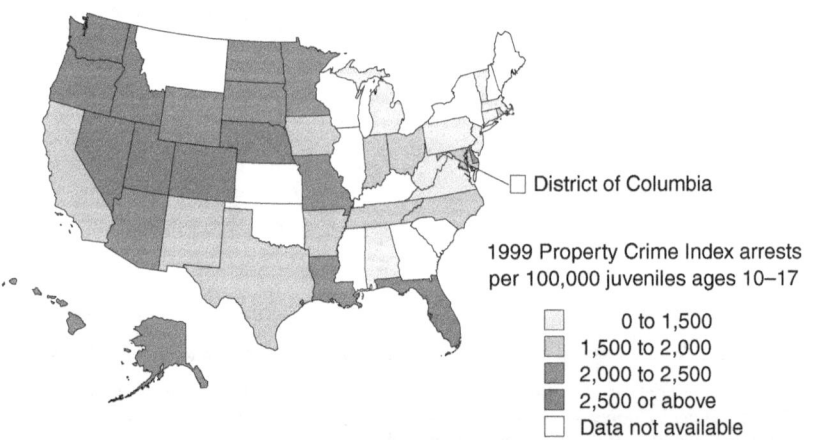

District of Columbia

1999 Property Crime Index arrests per 100,000 juveniles ages 10–17

- 0 to 1,500
- 1,500 to 2,000
- 2,000 to 2,500
- 2,500 or above
- Data not available

Property Crime Index arrest rates are a barometer of the flow of youth into the juvenile justice system

The Property Crime Index is dominated by the high-volume crime category of larceny-theft. For juveniles, shoplifting is the most common offense in this category. The Index also includes the crimes of home burglary, auto theft, and arson—all serious crimes. Therefore, to assess the nature of juvenile property crimes within a jurisdiction, one must consider the categories individually. Nevertheless, since much juvenile crime is property crime, juvenile Property Crime Index arrest rates are a good barometer of the flow of juveniles into the juvenile justice system. In 1998, the national juvenile property crime arrest rate was 2,130. The highest rate reported by a county was more than five times the national rate. Nearly three-fourths of reporting counties had rates below the national average. Half of all reporting counties had rates below 1,518.

In 1998, the counties with high Property Crime Index arrest rates did not necessarily have high Violent Crime Index arrest rates

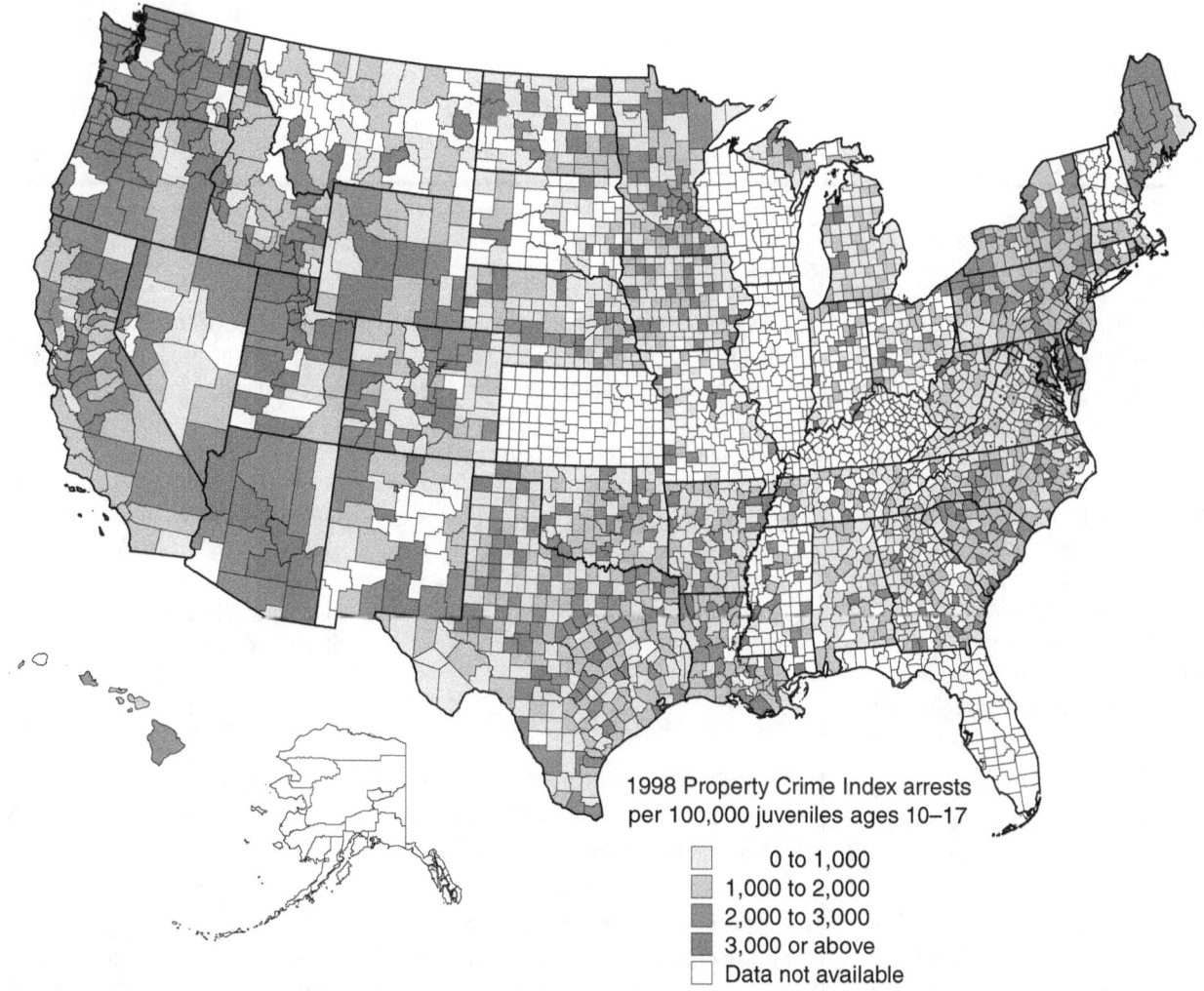

1998 Property Crime Index arrests per 100,000 juveniles ages 10–17

- 0 to 1,000
- 1,000 to 2,000
- 2,000 to 3,000
- 3,000 or above
- Data not available

Note: Rates were classified as "Data not available" when agencies with jurisdiction over more than 50% of their county's population did not report.

Data source: Analysis of arrest estimates from the Inter-university Consortium for Political and Social Research's *Uniform Crime Reporting Program data [United States]: County-level detailed arrest and offense data, 1998* [machine-readable data file] and population estimates from the U.S. Bureau of the Census' *Estimates of the population of counties by age and sex: 1990–1999* [machine-readable data files available online, released August 30, 2000].

Technical note

Although juvenile arrest rates may largely reflect juvenile behavior, many other factors can affect the magnitude of these rates. Arrest rates are calculated by dividing the number of youth arrests made in the year by the number of youth living in the jurisdiction. Therefore, jurisdictions that arrest a relatively large number of nonresident juveniles would have a higher arrest rate than jurisdictions where resident youth behave similarly. Jurisdictions (especially small ones) that are vacation destinations or that are centers for economic activity in a region may have arrest rates that reflect the behavior of nonresident youth more than that of resident youth.

Other factors that influence arrest rates in a given area include the attitudes of citizens toward crime, the policies of local law enforcement agencies, and the policies of other components of the justice system. In many areas, not all law enforcement agencies report their arrest data to the FBI. Rates for such areas are necessarily based on partial information and may not be accurate.

Comparisons of juvenile arrest rates across jurisdictions can be informative. Because of the factors noted, however, comparisons should be made with caution.

Arrest rate data source

Analysis of arrest data from unpublished FBI reports for 1980 through 1997 and from *Crime in the United States* reports for 1998 and 1999 (Washington, DC: U.S. Government Printing Office, 1999 and 2000, respectively); population data from the U.S. Bureau of the Census, *U.S. Population Estimates by Age, Sex, Race, and Hispanic Origin: 1980 to 1999* [machine-readable data files available online, released April 11, 2000].

Acknowledgments

This Bulletin was written by Howard N. Snyder, Director of Systems Research at the National Center for Juvenile Justice, with funds provided by OJJDP to support the Juvenile Justice Statistics and Systems Development Program (cooperative agreement number 95–JN–FX–K008). The author gratefully acknowledges the assistance provided by the FBI's Criminal Justice Information Services Division, specifically, Ken Candell and Maryvictoria Pyne.

References

Snyder, H.N. 1999. The overrepresentation of juvenile crime proportions in robbery clearance statistics. *Journal of Quantitative Criminology* 15(2):151–161.

Snyder, H.N. 2000. *Sexual Assault of Young Children as Reported to Law Enforcement: Victim, Incident, and Offender Characteristics.* BJS Report. Washington, DC: U.S. Department of Justice, Office of Justice Programs, Bureau of Justice Statistics.

www.ingramcontent.com/pod-product-compliance
Lightning Source LLC
Chambersburg PA
CBHW080623180526
45168CB00007B/3036